AHEAD
LOOK
classroom COURSE

upper intermediate

STUDENTS' BOOK

JON NAUNTON

ANDY HOPKINS

JOCELYN POTTER

Look Ahead: a partnership between

 BBC English

 The British Council

 University of Cambridge Local Examinations Syndicate (UCLES)

 Longman ELT

 with the cooperation of the Council of Europe

Longman

Welcome to Look Ahead Upper Intermediate

1 Look at the pictures of some of the people who talk about their work and lives in the Documentary sections of this book.

Documentary sections provide the answers to the clues on these pages. Fill in the missing letters in the puzzle.

1 D _ _ _ _ _
2 _ O _ _ _ _ _
3 _ _ C _
4 _ _ _ _ _ _ _ _ _ U _ _ _
5 _ _ M _ _ _
6 _ E _ _ _ _ _
7 _ _ _ _ N _ _ _
8 _ _ _ _ _ T _ _ _
9 _ A _ _ _ _
10 _ _ R _ _ _ _ _
11 _ Y _ _ _ _

1 What is this man's hobby?

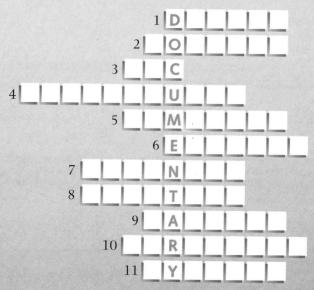

3 Where does this woman work?

6 This man works at the Bank of ..... .

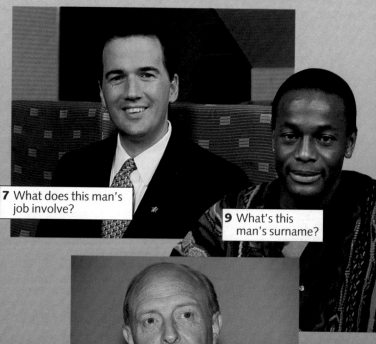

7 What does this man's job involve?

9 What's this man's surname?

8 What has been this man's passion for many years?

2 What is this woman's surname?

4 This man almost drowned in which river?

5 Where is this woman going to teach English?

10 Where does this man work?

11 What is the name of the school in Unit 2?

2 Which of these five objects and places would you associate with five of the people shown in the Documentaries?

A challenging reward

B

C

D

E

3 📼 Listen to five short extracts from the Documentaries. Which of the people from Exercise 1 is speaking?

4 Work in groups. Which units are you most looking forward to using? Which ones do you think will be the most challenging?

5 In *Look Ahead Upper Intermediate* there is a literature element. Look at the contents chart on pages 2 to 5 under the heading 'Reading'. Find out which authors wrote about the following.

1 A man who loved gold.
2 Education in the future.
3 The end of the world.
4 Tricks that our memory can play.
5 An unhappy experience at work.

Now answer these questions.

1 Which pieces are poetry?
2 What is the connection between the pieces of literature and the units in which they appear?

Focus

TOPIC
- International connections

GRAMMAR
- Present simple
- Present progressive
- Active and stative verbs

SKILLS
- Reading: people's opinions
- Speaking: giving opinions
- Listening: individual's opinions

Something in common?

GETTING STARTED

1 Look at the pictures. What do they have in common?

READING

2 Read the texts and match them with the pictures.

1 ❝I think that the United Nations does a good job. I mean, we haven't had a world war now for a long time, have we? I believe that it's stupid to fight; it seems to me it's much better to solve problems around the conference table. Countries don't fight and argue so much now.❞   PAUL from Canada

2 ❝The Olympic Games? Well, I'm thinking about going to the next ones. I love athletics. I'm a keen athlete myself and I want to go once in my life. They really bring people from all over the world together. Of course, politics are too involved in the Games nowadays. The Games belong to the athletes, not the politicians.❞   KIRI from New Zealand

3 ❝I feel it is a good thing to have a united Europe for business. In fact, I study international trade at university. But European culture is a different thing! Wherever you go in Europe there are burger bars where the food tastes the same, discos where you hear the same music and see everyone under twenty-five in the same clothes. I absolutely detest this! Maybe I'm being stupid, but I want countries and regions to keep their identity.❞   OLIVIER from France

4 ❝I come from Cracow in Poland, but at the moment I'm studying English in London. I've been here for three months. Now I know people from all over the world. I often think about how similar we all are. There's no big difference between us really. I believe that age, education and background are more important than nationality. I think of myself as a global citizen.❞   DANUTA from Poland

D

DISCOVERING LANGUAGE

6 Read the texts again and find these words.

believe   seem   love   want   belong
hear   detest   know

1 Which tense are the words used in? Can they be used in the progressive?
2 Which words deal with beliefs, possession, emotions and the senses?

3 Read the texts again and answer these questions.

1 What is the role of the United Nations (UN)? Does Paul think the UN has been successful? Do you agree?
2 How interested is Kiri in the Olympic Games? How interested are you? To what extent do you think they are political?
3 How European is Olivier? Do you feel as though you belong to something which is bigger than your country?
4 What worries Olivier about European culture? Do you share his views?
5 Why is Danuta so sympathetic to other cultures?

REVIEWING LANGUAGE

4 Look at the pairs of sentences. How does the change in tense affect their meaning?

1 A *I study international trade.*
  B *I'm studying English in London.*
2 A *It's stupid to fight.*
  B *Maybe I'm being stupid.*
3 A *I often think about how similar we all are.*
  B *I'm thinking about going to the next ones.*

Which sentences, A or B, describe temporary states, temporary activities or temporary mental activity?

5 Make questions for these answers, using the correct form of the verbs in brackets.

How nice it is here. (think)
What are you thinking about?

1 I'm a reporter on a local newspaper. (do)
2 It's a book about mountaineering; I started it last week. (read)
3 No, because there's nowhere to park near the office. (drive)
4 Maria? She's really nice. (think)
5 At the Ramada Hotel. It's near the centre. (stay)
6 I'll turn the TV up so you can hear it. (say)

7 Change the verb in brackets into an appropriate form.

I [1]..... (write) this letter because it [2]..... (seem) to me that everywhere I [3]..... (go) in my country it [4]..... (lose) its identity. I [5]..... (live) in a little town where I [6]..... (own) a small shop, but even this town [7]..... (change) before my eyes. In fact they [8]..... (build) a burger bar where my favourite restaurant used to be. Our culture [9]..... (belong) to everyone, but nobody [10]..... (want) to do anything to preserve it. I [11]..... (understand) that we [12]..... (need) progress, but not if it [13]..... (cost) too much. Perhaps I [14]..... (be) difficult, but in my eyes every town centre nowadays [15]..... (look) the same.

LISTENING

8 📼 Listen to Kiri talking about some other topics from the reading texts. Does she feel positive, negative or unsure about:

1 the United Nations?
2 the European Union?
3 going to Europe?

⟳ COMPARING CULTURES

9 Work in groups. Discuss these questions.

1 How important to you is the individual identity of your town or region? What traditions is it well-known for? Do they need to be preserved?
2 Does your country belong to an international political or trading group? If yes, what benefits has this association brought?
3 How do you and citizens of your country generally feel about the influence of foreign cultures? Is there one particular culture which you think is too dominant?
4 How many of the people in the group feel like, or would like to be 'global citizens'?

Focus

TOPIC
• Political systems

GRAMMAR
• Past simple
• Present perfect
• Present perfect progressive

SKILLS
• Listening: a monologue
• Speaking: an interview

A question of trust

GETTING STARTED

1 Which of the people in this list would you trust the most and which the least?

a university professor   a car salesperson   a police officer
a famous sportsperson   a priest   a distant cousin
a doctor   a politician

🖵 Documentary

LISTENING

2 Britain has three main political parties: Conservative, Labour and Liberal Democrat. Before you listen, find out what people in your class know about these parties and what they stand for.

3 🖭 Listen and read. Neil Kinnock (above), the ex-leader of the Labour party, talks about the British political system. Correct the facts and figures in bold type in this summary.

Parliament is divided into two houses: the House of Commons, which is entirely elected – everybody in the House of Commons is an elected Member of Parliament, and they're elected from **615** constituencies in the United Kingdom. Constituencies vary a little in size, but most of them are around about **50,000** electors. The political parties put candidates up for election and the election is decided by 'first past the post', that is to say, the candidate with the most votes gets elected. The **Senate** is a non-elected chamber of the parliament and its roots go back for **1,600** years.

4 Which words in the summary mean:

1 the people who want to be elected?
2 someone who sits in the House of Commons?
3 the people who vote?
4 geographical areas that elect one person to Parliament?

READING

5 Read the comparison of 'first past the post' with 'proportional representation'. How 'fair' is the British system?

Voting values

MANY countries have a proportional system, that is, the number of seats a party gains in parliament depends upon the percentage of people who vote for it. In the 1992 British General Election the Liberal Democrats won only 20 seats under the first past the post system even though 18 % of the electorate voted for them. Under a proportional system they would have won about 118 seats. The first past the post system meant it 'cost' about 40,000 votes to elect a Labour or Conservative MP, but 300,000 for a Liberal Democrat!

LISTENING

6 🖭 Listen to Neil Kinnock talking about the House of Lords, and answer these questions.

1 Some 'peers', members of the House of Lords, are hereditary. In other words, they inherit their seat in the House of Lords. How does Mr Kinnock feel about the situation?
2 How would he change the situation?

7 📼 Listen to Mr Kinnock describing the role of the monarchy (the King or Queen) and answer these questions.

1 How long has Britain had a constitutional monarchy?
2 Who writes the Queen's speech and what does it contain?

↻ COMPARING CULTURES

8 What would you tell a foreigner about the political system in your own country? Make notes about the following, then use them to describe your political system.

1 Who is in charge.   4 The main political parties.
2 Your parliament.   5 A famous politician.
3 The electoral system.

LISTENING

9 📼 Listen to Neil Kinnock talking about his political career and answer the questions.

1 When did his political life begin?
2 Write the dates of the elections he has fought.
3 Has he ever made any mistakes?
4 What regrets does he have?

REVIEWING LANGUAGE

10 Look at the pairs of sentences and answer the questions.

   A *I've made mistakes in my political career.*
   B *I made mistakes in my political career.*
1 In which sentence is his political career finished?
2 In which sentence does he still have a political career?
3 Which tense is used in each case?

   C *I've written a speech this morning.*
   D *I've been writing a speech.*
4 In which sentence is the result emphasised?
5 In which sentence is the activity emphasised?
6 In which sentence is the action definitely complete?
7 In which sentence may the action be incomplete?

   E *I've known Neil Kinnock for years.*
   F *We've been working together for a long time.*
8 Which tense is used in each sentence?
9 Why can't we use the present perfect progressive in sentence E?

Study what Carole says in sentence G and answer the questions.

   G *'Your voice sounds tired, Paul. Have you been making a speech?'*
10 Is Paul making a speech now?
11 Why does Carole think Paul made a speech earlier?

11 Complete the text about Screaming Lord Sutch by changing the verbs in brackets into an appropriate tense.

Lord Sutch is a rock musician with a difference. He [1] ..... (perform) for years and his outrageous stage act continues to shock audiences. He [2] ..... (make) two successful albums. However, it is his political activities that [3] ..... (make) him famous; and if he sometimes looks tired, it may be because he [4] ..... (fight) an election! He [5] ..... (fight) over thirty elections since he [6] ..... (start) in 1962, but he [7] ..... (never win). Some people say he [8] ..... (give) politics a bad name in his search for publicity, but major parties [9] ..... (adopt) some of his early policies, for example, giving people the vote at eighteen and the abolition of a famous exam.

12 You are interviewing Screaming Lord Sutch. Write questions for his answers.

1 In 1962.
2 More than thirty.
3 No, never.
4 For years.

Think of three more questions and answers to continue the interview.

SPEAKING

13 Work in pairs. Invent an interview with a political figure or other famous person from your own country and act out your interviews.

Focus

TOPIC
- Political opinions

FUNCTIONS
- Giving opinions
- Agreeing/ disagreeing

SKILLS
- Listening: a discussion
- Speaking: discussing a questionnaire/ discussing a party manifesto/giving a speech
- Reading: a speech
- Writing: a speech

SPEECH PATTERNS
- Giving opinions: stress and intonation

QUESTIONNAIRE

So where do you stand?

Mark the boxes A–E according to your opinions.

1 Everyone should be free to choose their health care and education. ☐

2 Stricter punishments stop crime. ☐

3 It is important for our country's security to have strong armed forces. ☐

4 We worry far too much about the environment. ☐

5 Children are influenced by violence on TV. ☐

KEY

A = completely agree   D = slightly disagree
B = agree   E = totally disagree
C = neither agree nor disagree

Discussing points of view

READING

1 Read the questionnaire but *don't* answer it yet.

LISTENING

2 📼 Now listen to Amanda, Roger and George discussing the first question. What choices do you think they made?

3 📼 Listen again and answer these questions.

1 Why do Roger and George disagree about private health care?
2 What problem does Amanda identify with Roger's point about 'freedom of choice'?
3 What imaginary situation does Roger ask the other two to consider?
4 Why does Amanda find the question about health and education difficult to answer?
5 How strong are George's political principles?
6 Does anyone win the argument?

FOCUS ON FUNCTIONS

4 📼 **Listen again. Which of the expressions in the list below do you hear?**

GIVING YOUR OPINION
In my opinion ...
From my point of view ...
As far as I'm concerned ...
As I see it ...
I'm for/against ...

GIVING SOMEONE ELSE'S OPINION
According to ...

AGREEING
I (quite/completely) agree.
I agree with you.
That's right.
Exactly.
I think so (too).
Absolutely.

DISAGREEING
I don't think so.
I don't agree (with) ...
But surely, ...
Certainly not.
I take your point, but ...
I totally disagree.
That's nonsense.

SPEECH PATTERNS

5 📺 Listen and repeat these sentences from the conversation. Which words are stressed?

1 As I see it, it's up to the state to help.
2 In my opinion, that's the most important thing.

FOCUS ON FUNCTIONS

6 Look at these ways of agreeing. How do we form the short answer when we want to agree with what has just been said?

A: I think the government is responsible.
B: So do I./I do too.
A: I don't think it's fair.
B: Neither do I./I don't either.

7 Write replies agreeing with these statements.

1 A: I don't agree with him.
  B: I . . . . .
2 A: I feel really tired.
  B: So . . . . .
3 A: I am confused.
  B: I . . . . .
4 A: I didn't watch the programme.
  B: . . . . .

SPEAKING

8 Complete the questionnaire and then discuss the results with as many people in the class as possible. Make a note of other people's choices. Use as many of the expressions from Exercise 4 as you can.

READING

9 Read this short speech by Fabrizia from Italy. There are some mistakes in it. Work in pairs or groups to correct the text.

❝Hello, everybody. I am here on behalf of the New Generation Party. We are believing that people have to wait too long for to vote. They are enough old to vote at sixteen. It is more democratic. Old people over sixty shouldn't vote because they are out of touch. Also, young people should have a salary from the government even when they are studying. Then they can have their own flats. For too long they have had to live with their parents.

We are also going to abolish the military service. According to me it is a crazy thing that young people have to make it. We will ban the nuclear power too. I am agree with generating electricity from the sun. We also stand for animal rights. There will be no more experiences on animals for testing new pharmaceuticals. From my opinion this is a scandal and must stop.

A vote for us is a vote for the future because the future depends from us.❞

SPEAKING

10 Work in pairs and discuss Fabrizia's points of view. Would you vote for her?

11 Group yourselves into two or three political parties according to the views you expressed in the questionnaire.

1 Agree a name for your party.
2 Make notes about your party's beliefs and reasons for these beliefs.

WRITING

12 In your groups, use the corrected version of Fabrizia's speech as a guide and write the speech for your party.

SPEAKING

13 Choose someone from your group to read the speech to the rest of the class. Hold a secret ballot and decide which person/party makes the best speech.

Grammar reference

1 The present simple
- We use the present simple to talk about states, habits, routines and facts about the world.
  EXAMPLES: *I'm German; I come from Berlin.*
  I get up at seven o'clock every morning.
  Lions eat meat.
- Adverbs of frequency, e.g. *sometimes, often, never*, are often used with the present simple.
- We also use the present simple to talk about timetables and programmes of events.
  EXAMPLE: *When does the next train to Cambridge leave? It leaves at half past four.*

2 The present progressive
The present progressive is used to talk about:
- temporary activities or states in the present.
  EXAMPLES: *Someone is walking towards the house.*
  Bob and I are having golf lessons.
- fixed future plans, often with a future time adverbial.
  EXAMPLE: *I'm having lunch with James next Tuesday.*
See also Grammar reference 15.3 for the use of *always* with the present progressive.

3 The present simple or present progressive?
- There are some verbs which are hardly ever used in the progressive form. They deal with states, emotions or senses which remain permanent:
  Verbs of cognition: *believe, know, understand, mean, remember.*
  Verbs of possession: *own, belong.*
  Verbs of liking and disliking: *like, love, hate, detest, prefer.*
  Other verbs: *seem, hear, need, want, cost.*
  EXAMPLES: *I know what you mean.*
  This pen belongs to me.
- There are other verbs which can be used in the simple or progressive form, but with some change of meaning: *be, think, taste, smell.*
  EXAMPLES: *Paul is stupid.* (He's stupid all the time.)
  Paul is being stupid. (At the moment.)
  What do you think? (What is your opinion?)
  What are you thinking? (What is going on in your mind at the moment?)
  The progressive forms of the verbs *taste* and *smell* can only be used to describe actions:
  She's tasting the soup to see if it needs more salt.
  (But: *The flowers smell nice.*)

4 The present perfect simple
We use the present perfect simple to talk about:
- actions and situations that began in the past but are not finished.
  EXAMPLES: *He has been a politician for twenty years.* (He is still in politics.)
  I've been here since five o'clock. (I came here at five o'clock and I'm still here.)
- finished actions and events when the time is not specified, especially recent events with a result in the present.
  EXAMPLES: *This is the news. Moronian troops have invaded Ruritania. The invasion took place at three o'clock this morning.* (Past simple when specific time is mentioned.)
  The flight from Milan has just arrived.
  Oh no! I've lost my keys!
- people's experiences in their life up to now, often with *ever* and *never*.
  EXAMPLES: *She has been a diplomat and a university professor.*
  I've never eaten Chinese food.
  'Have you ever' questions are often used when people are discussing experiences.
  EXAMPLE: *Have you ever been to Italy? Yes, I have. Where did you go?* (past simple for specific detail)
  I visited Venice, Florence and Pisa.
- actions in an unfinished period of time, often with *yet, already* or *so far*.
  EXAMPLE: *I've written three letters so far this morning.*

5 The present perfect progressive
We use the present perfect progressive to talk about:
- activities which started in the past and are still continuing.
  EXAMPLE: *She's been studying French for six months.*
- continuous actions that recently stopped but have a result in the present.
  EXAMPLE: *You've been crying, haven't you?* (I know because your eyes are red.)

Progress check Unit 1

1 Complete the biography by choosing the most appropriate form of the verbs.

Mrs Winifred Weaver ([1]is/has been/was involved) in politics ever since she ([2]was/has been) a student. She ([3]went/has been) to Hull University, where she ([4]studied/has studied) agriculture. On the first day of her course, she ([5]joined/has joined) the Labour Party. The first time she ([6]spoke/has spoken) in a debate she ([7]forgot/has forgotten) what she ([8]wanted/has wanted) to say. Since then she ([9]always prepared/has always prepared/has always been preparing) her speeches in detail. She ([10]had/has had) a distinguished career in politics, and ([11]represents/ has represented) her constituency for thirty years. Despite a busy life, Mrs Weaver ([12]has written/wrote) several influential books. For the past few months she ([13]has written/has been writing) her memoirs, although she insists her political career ([14]isn't finishing/hasn't finished) yet.

2 Complete this letter to an English farmer by changing the verbs in brackets into an appropriate form.

I [1]..... (write) to ask if I can pick apples for you this season. My cousin Raymond [2]..... (work) for you last year and [3]..... (enjoy) himself. Also, I [4]..... (want) to improve my English as I [5]..... (think) of studying abroad.

I [6]..... (be) twenty and [7]..... (come) from the west of France; I [8]..... (belong) to a family of French farmers. We [9]..... (own) a farm and [10]..... (produce) cheese and yoghurt.

I [11]..... (study) at agricultural college for three years and I [12]..... (love) working outside. Before that I [13]..... (be) at school. I [14]..... (hope) you [15]..... (not think) that I [16]..... (be) 'pushy', but I would like to work on your farm. Of course I [17]..... (understand) if you [18]..... (not need) anyone this year.

3 Complete the dialogue below. Follow the example.

PAUL: Hello, Anna. I /not see you /long time.
Hello, Anna. I haven't seen you for a long time.
ANNA: I/just come back/Italy.
PAUL: You/be/on holiday?
ANNA: No. I/work/tour company.
PAUL: You/have/good time?
ANNA: Well, it/be/hard work, but really enjoyable. You/ever go/Italy?
PAUL: No, I/not there yet/but I/love to go. How long/you/be/there?
ANNA: Six months. By the way, you/lose/weight/since /last time/I /see you?
PAUL: Yes. I/give up/eating chocolate/cakes. In fact, I/not have any/since Christmas.

4 Complete the discussion with these expressions.

But surely   I take your point   I quite agree
As I see it   According to

GEORGE: [1]..... Danuta, we should all be global citizens.
KAREN: [2]..... .
GEORGE: That's too romantic. [3]..... , we should be proud of our national characteristics.
KAREN: Of course. [4]..... you'd agree that we should understand each other's cultures?
GEORGE: [5]..... , Karen, but isn't it our differences that make us interesting?

5 Complete these sentences with a word on the topic of political elections.

1 There are two political ..... in the United States: the Democrats and the Republicans.
2 Mrs Biggs was the winning ..... and was elected to Parliament.
3 There are about 60,000 ....., or voters, in each constituency.
4 The political system where a king or queen is the head of state is called a ..... .
5 The ..... is all the people who are allowed to vote in the entire country.

2 Making the grade

Dos and don'ts

Focus

TOPICS
- Schools
- Rules and regulations

GRAMMAR
- *Make, let, allow, be supposed to, have to, must*
- Expressing obligation

SKILLS
- Listening: monologues
- Speaking: explaining rules

VOCABULARY DEVELOPMENT
- Verbs related to exams

GETTING STARTED

1 How important is it to have rules and strict discipline in schools?

🖾 Documentary

LISTENING

2 Before you listen, say what you think these are:

a public school   a private school   a boarding school
a state school   a grammar school   a comprehensive school

1 Which of the schools are free, i.e. paid by the government and which do you have to pay to attend?
2 Which schools have entrance examinations?
3 How old do you think are first formers and sixth formers who attend a grammar school?

3 🔊 Listen to a sixth former and her teachers talking about Wycombe High School and answer these questions.

1 What kind of school is Wycombe High School? How does the sixth former explain/define it?
2 What percentage of candidates are accepted?
3 How many grammar schools are there in England?
4 How many pupils does the school have?
5 What is the relationship between the main school and the sixth form?

A

B

4 🔊 Listen to the sixth former and teacher talking about the rules about uniforms. Which year is the pupil in Picture A in? What rules has the sixth former in Picture B broken?

5 🖭 **Listen and answer the questions.**

1 What should girls do when a teacher comes into the classroom?
2 What freedom do sixth formers have?
3 What are the head teacher's reasons for not allowing the girls to go to the bottom of the field?
4 What are the rules for:
   a) the library?   b) the study room?
   c) the common room?
5 Why does the head think rules are important?

DISCOVERING LANGUAGE

6 Look at the sentences below using active and passive forms of *make, let* and *allow*. Tick the correct ones and then complete the chart and answer the questions.

ACTIVE
A *They **make** us **to wear** a uniform.*
B *They **make** us **wear** a uniform.*
C *They **let** us **to wear** jewellery.*
D *They **let** us **wear** jewellery.*
E *They **allow** us **to wear** jewellery.*

PASSIVE
F *We are **made wear** a uniform.*
G *We are **made to wear** a uniform.*
H *We are **let to wear** jewellery.*
I *We are **allowed to wear** jewellery.*

		Infinitive with *to*	Infinitive without *to*
MAKE	active		✔
	passive		
LET	active		
	passive		
ALLOW	active		
	passive		

1 Which passive verb is *not* possible?
2 Which two verbs have the same meaning?

7 Complete Dominic's description of his school by changing the form of the verbs, where necessary.

'I hate school. Every morning the teachers [1]..... (make) us get up at six o'clock and run five kilometres. Afterwards all the pupils [2]..... (make) have a cold shower. The teachers never [3]..... (allow) us to go to the nearest village. Every Sunday we [4]..... (make) write a long letter home, but we [5]..... (not allow) complain about anything. Afterwards, they [6]..... (let) us watch television for two hours.'

REVIEWING LANGUAGE

8 Look at the sentences below. What is the difference in the strength of the three ways of expressing obligation?

A *We **have to** pass an exam before we enter the school.*
B *They**'re supposed to** keep the hair out of their eyes.*
C *Girls **must** walk on the left at all times.*

Which sentence expresses:

1 a strict rule?
2 a simple requirement or duty?
3 a recommended way of behaviour?

SPEAKING

9 Work in pairs.

Student A: Imagine that you are explaining some rules and duties to a new student or colleague. Tell him/her six things he/she needs to know about what to wear, being on time, doing homework, behaviour in general. Decide whether you are describing strict rules, rules that might be broken, simple requirements or duties. Find out from your partner what his/her last place was like.

Student B: Turn to page 128. Ask and answer the questions.

DEVELOPING VOCABULARY

10 Look at these two sentences from the Documentary.

a) We have to *pass an exam* before we can enter the school.
b) The girls tend to *sit an exam* at twelve in their primary schools.

Which verbs can you put in front of *an exam*?

take   set   fail   mark   do   revise for
have got   not succeed

Complete the sentences with appropriate verbs.

1 She is [1]..... an important examination tomorrow. If she [2]..... it, she'll get a place at medical school, but if she [3]..... , she'll have to try again next year.
2 Next month I [1]..... my final examinations so I am going to [2]..... them by getting up early and studying for two hours every day. Last year they [3]..... really difficult ones and lots of people [4]..... and had to [5]..... them all again. I don't want that to happen to me!

Different systems

Focus

TOPICS
• School subjects
• Exams

GRAMMAR
• *Although, despite*

FUNCTIONS
• Summarising
• Asking for repetition
• Showing understanding
• Picking up on an earlier point

SKILLS
• Listening: a conversation
• Reading: a newspaper article
• Speaking: explaining and clarifying

SPEECH PATTERNS
• Recognising falling intonation

GETTING STARTED

1 **In your opinion what is the most important thing about education: creating good citizens, preparing people for life, or creating a workforce?**

↻ COMPARING CULTURES

2 **Work in pairs. Discuss the following.**
In most countries there are examinations you have to pass before you can go on to higher education. In England you have to pass two subjects at 'A' (Advanced) level. What is the situation in your countries?

LISTENING

3 **Joanna is explaining to Malcolm how the International Baccalaureate works. Before you listen, discuss these questions.**
1 Look at the list of subjects that may be studied for the International Baccalaureate (IB). Which ones did/do you study at school or in your country?
2 Are there any subjects which you feel are missing or are a waste of time?

4 🖭 **Listen to Joanna and Malcolm's conversation and answer these questions.**
1 How many subjects must students offer?
2 Can they take more than one subject in each group?
3 Is it possible not to study mathematics or any one group of subjects?
4 What do HL and SL stand for?
5 What second choice must students make after they have chosen the subjects they wish to study?
6 What do you think of the IB? How similar is it to school-leaving qualifications in your countries?
7 Which subjects would you choose to do at Higher and Subsidiary Level?

SPEECH PATTERNS

5 **Now answer these questions.**
1 How do we know that Joanna is making a special effort to be clear and patient?
2 How does Malcolm know it is all right to interrupt, ask a question, or to make an encouraging sound?

CURRICULUM AND EXAMINATION

The curriculum consists of six subject groups, accompanied by three other central and fundamental programmes.

Group 1 Language A1 (first language) including the study of selections from World Literature.

Group 2 Language B (second language) or a second language A1.

Group 3 Individuals and Societies: History, Geography, Economics, Philosophy, Psychology, Social Anthropology, Organisation and Management Studies.

Group 4 Experimental Sciences: Biology, Chemistry HL, General Chemistry SL, Applied Chemistry SL, Physics, Environmental Systems.

Group 5 Mathematics: Mathematics HL and SL, Mathematics with Computing SL, Mathematical Studies SL, Mathematics with Further Mathematics HL/SL.

Group 6 One of the following options:
a) Art/Design, Music, Latin, Classical Greek, Computing Studies.
b) A School-based Syllabus approved by the International Baccalaureate Organisation (IBO).

Alternatively a candidate may offer instead of a third modern language, a second subject from Individuals and

Taken from *The International Baccalaureate*, 1992

FOCUS ON FUNCTIONS

6 📻 **Listen again to Joanna and Malcolm. How are these functions expressed?**

1 Summarising what you think has been said.
2 Asking for someone to repeat an explanation.
3 Showing that you finally understand.
4 Picking up and continuing an earlier point.

SPEAKING

7 Work in pairs.
Student A: Listen to the information about the English educational system which your partner will give you. Ask questions to make sure you fully understand.
Student B: Turn to page 128 and tell your partner about the English educational system.

READING

8 Before you read, discuss these questions.

1 What are the advantages of studying in an international school?
2 How well would people get on with each other? Would some nationalities do better than others?

9 Read the newspaper article and find out if these statements are true or false. Correct the false ones.

1 The Lycée is just for secondary school students.
2 Students can choose the school-leaving qualification they try for.
3 There are ten or more nationalities in the school.
4 Most of the time, pupils are taught in French.
5 The school is open to all-comers.
6 It has exceptionally good academic results.

DISCOVERING LANGUAGE

10 Look at the sentences in bold type in the article. Then answer these questions.

1 Would we usually expect to find international sections in a state school?
2 Some students join the school speaking no French. Is it surprising that they can follow lessons in French and take the French *baccalauréat* just three years later?
3 Which words show that there is a contrast of ideas in the sentences?
4 How are *despite* and *although* different grammatically? What structures follow each form?

11 Join these ideas using *although* and *despite*.

1 He was extremely stupid. He passed his exams.
2 It is a state school. The students come from rich families.
3 Pupils study in France. Many choose foreign universities.

12 Think of three things you did/have done at school which were surprising or unexpected. Make sentences using *although* and *despite* and compare them with a partner.

Although I rarely did my homework, I was usually top of the class!

Learning together

At the Lycée International de Saint-Germain-en-Laye, near Versailles, French and foreign pupils study together from nursery school right through to the final school-leaving exams. These can either be an ordinary French *baccalauréat* or the newer international version. **Despite being a state school, St Germain has ten national sections;** the latest section, for Japanese, having opened this month. Throughout their schooling pupils attend their national section for six to eight hours a week, when they are taught by native speakers the language, literature and history of the country concerned. **Despite the fact that only half of the Lycée's 2,500 pupils are French, they all follow normal** French lessons together for much of the time. Jean-Pierre Maillard, the principal, says: '**Although roughly half of our pupils don't speak French when they arrive, they are able to sit the French baccalauréat, some only three years later.'**

The school is for the bright. Standards are high and the workload is heavy. Candidates are carefully selected and may be invited to go elsewhere if they fall behind. Not surprisingly, the Lycée is among the top ten in the unofficial *bac* results published in the monthly magazine *Le Monde de l'Education*. Some pupils become fluent in three or even four languages and many go to universities abroad. The UK is a popular choice and the British section is proud of its steady stream going to Oxford and Cambridge.

Strong images

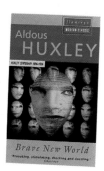

Focus

TOPIC
- Conditioning

SKILLS
- Reading: a literary extract
- Listening: a literary extract
- Speaking: a discussion/ telling a story
- Writing: a story

STYLE
- Similes

VOCABULARY DEVELOPMENT
- Positive/negative adjectives
- Verbs of *taking* and *holding*
- Verbs of *shouting*
- Adverbs of manner

1 Read this introduction to the extract from *Brave New World*.

Brave New World by Aldous Huxley is set in a future where people are biologically mass-produced and 'hatched' like chickens. Batches of people of different intellectual and physical abilities are produced according to society's needs and named after the letters of the Greek alphabet (*alpha, beta*, etc.). Families no longer exist and children are brought up in nurseries where they are conditioned to be good citizens. In this extract the person in charge, the Director of Hatcheries and Conditioning (the D.H.C.) demonstrates the process to some students.

READING

2 Before you read, discuss these questions.

1 How would you train a circus dog to jump through a burning hoop?
2 What would the different stages in the training process be?

3 Read the text and decide how similar the process is to the one for the circus dog.

1- The nurses stiffened to attention as the D.H.C. came in.
'Set out the books,' he said curtly.
In silence the nurses carried out his command. A row of children's books full of brightly coloured pictures was
5- set out in front of the children.
'Now bring in the children.'
They hurried out of the room and returned in a minute or two, each pushing a kind of trolley full of identical eight-month-old babies.
10- 'Put them down on the floor.'
The infants were unloaded. They were a Delta group all dressed in khaki.
'Now turn them so that they can see the flowers and books.'
15- Turned, the babies at once fell silent, then began to crawl towards the illustrated books. The crawling babies gurgled with pleasure and excitement.
The fastest crawlers had already reached them and touched the petals of the flowers and the pages of the
20- books. The Director waited until all were happily busy. Then, 'Watch carefully,' he said. And, lifting his hand, he gave the signal.
The Head Nurse pulled a switch and there was a violent explosion. A siren shrieked and alarm bells rang
25- loudly. The children screamed with terror.
'And now,' the Director shouted (for the noise was deafening), 'now we proceed to reinforce the lesson with a small electric shock.'
He waved his hand again, and the Head Nurse
30- pressed a second lever. The screaming became louder and desperate. Their arms and legs moved as if they were being pulled by unseen wires.

78

4 Now answer these questions.

1 What do you think will happen when the babies are shown the books and flowers again?
2 How would you quickly explain this conditioning process?
3 Which lines convey a positive/negative emotional situation? Which words help to convey these different moods?
4 Which simile (comparison) does the writer use to help us understand the way the children moved?

LISTENING

5 In the next part of the story the D.H.C. explains why Delta children are conditioned not to like flowers. Before you listen, can you think of any possible explanation?

6 📟 Now listen for answers to these questions.

1 Why had Deltas once been conditioned to love nature and the countryside?
2 Why was this considered to be unsatisfactory?
3 What was the aim of the new conditioning?
4 What were Deltas conditioned to love and hate?

SPEAKING

7 Work in pairs and discuss these questions.

1 Are people in today's society conditioned to behave in a certain way?
2 What methods are used?

FOCUS ON STYLE

8 We use similes when we describe something by comparing it with something else, like this example.

Her face was white. Snow is white.
= *Her face was as white as snow.*

Make simple similes from these prompts.

1 The night was coal-black.
2 The carpet was blood-red.
3 The water was ice-cold.
4 Her hair was corn-gold.

9 Look at this simile.

*Their arms and legs moved **as if** they were being pulled by unseen wires.*

Match these split sentences to form extended similes.

1 The wave was so powerful, it was as if ...
2 The desert was so hot, it was as if ...
3 The prison cell was dark and airless, it was as if ...
4 The flight was so terrifying, it was as if ...

a) I was in the middle of a nightmare.
b) a giant hand was picking up the boat.
c) we were in an oven.
d) he was shut in a coffin.

DEVELOPING VOCABULARY

10 Using your dictionaries, put the words in the list in the categories a)–e) below.

grab   yell   grateful   weakly   terrified   grip
scream   relieved   exhausted   shriek
painfully   safe   grasp   petrified

a) adverbs of manner
b) negative adjectives/adjectives to do with fear
c) positive adjectives
d) ways of shouting
e) ways of taking and holding

SPEAKING

11 Look at the pictures which describe what happened to Monika when she was learning to ski. Work in pairs or groups and construct the story. Use the questions below to help you.

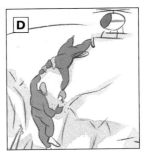

- How did she feel as she went up the mountain?
- What happened to Monika halfway down?
- What did the instructor do?
- What was it like in the crevasse?
- What did she do to try and get help?
- What did she do when she heard the rescuers?
- How did she hold the hand that rescued her?
- How did she feel in the helicopter?

WRITING

12 Write the story, using the notes you made in Exercise 11. Try to use some vocabulary and similes from Exercises 8, 9 and 10.

Grammar reference

1 Have to

- We use *have to* to talk about necessity.
  EXAMPLES: *You **have to pass an entrance exam** to get into that school.*
  *I can't stay long, I'm afraid. I **have to be at the airport** at four o'clock.*

- We often use *have got to* instead of *have to*. It is less formal.
  EXAMPLE: *I'm sorry, I**'ve got to go** now.*

2 Have to and must

- We use both *have to* and *must* to talk about obligations, duties and rules. Sometimes they are used interchangeably but we often use *must* to express the authority of the speaker (or writer), and *have to* to express the authority of someone else – when another person has made the rules. *Must* is often used for a stronger obligation.
  EXAMPLES: *Pupils who wish to borrow a book **must** show their library ticket.* (Teacher talking to pupils.)
  *If you want to borrow a book, you **have to** show your library ticket.* (Pupil explaining the rule to another pupil.)

- Only use *You must* if you are expressing your authority, or are angry with someone.
  EXAMPLE: *You **must** be more careful in future!*

3 Negatives of have to and must

The negative forms of *have to* and *must* have different meanings.

- *Don't have to* (or *haven't got to*) means 'it isn't necessary' or 'there is no obligation'.
  EXAMPLES: *It's only three o'clock. We **don't have to** leave yet.*
  *Pupils in the sixth form **don't have to** wear a uniform.*

- *Must not* is a negative imperative used for prohibitions. Its meaning is similar to *Don't*.
  EXAMPLE: *You **mustn't** park here!*

4 Be supposed to

- *Be supposed to* expresses a recommended way of behaving or a rule which the speaker doesn't think is very important.
  EXAMPLES: *You**'re supposed to** wait there until your name is called.*
  *We**'re supposed to** sign in at Reception, but I never bother.*

5 Make, let, allow and may

- *To make somebody do something* means to force or compel them.
  EXAMPLE: *Her father **made her stay** at home.*
  In the passive form, we use the infinitive with *to*.
  EXAMPLE: *She **was made to stay** at home.*

- *Let* and *allow* are both used to express permission. Notice that *allow* is followed by the infinitive with *to*.
  EXAMPLES: *They **let** him **watch** the late night film.*
  *They **allowed** him **to watch** the late night film.*
  In the passive, we can only use *allow*, not *let*.
  EXAMPLE: *He **was allowed to watch** the late night film.*

6 Although and despite

- *Although* and *Despite the fact that* both operate as conjunctions and have the same meaning. They introduce a clause containing a subject and a verb.
  EXAMPLES: ***Although** he finds maths difficult, he is making good progress.*
  ***Despite the fact that** he finds maths difficult, he is making good progress.*
  These sentences mean the same as:
  He finds maths difficult, but is making good progress.
  but they place more emphasis on the contrast between the two ideas.

- *Despite* is a preposition with the same meaning. It must be followed by a noun, pronoun or *-ing* form.
  EXAMPLE: ***Despite** doing badly in his exams, he managed to get into university.*

Talkback

Just deserts

1 Work in groups. Discuss these statements about prisons and punishment.

1 The object of prisons is to reform and educate criminals.
2 The main purpose of prison is to show society's anger and to punish the criminal.
3 Prisons are universities of crime.
4 The punishment must fit the crime.

2 Now read this text about a new approach to dealing with young criminals. Does it support your views in Exercise 1?

IN BRITAIN, young people who have committed serious crimes have sometimes been sent abroad on long trips as part of their rehabilitation therapy. The victims of these crimes are often angry because they feel the young criminals are being rewarded, not punished.

It is expensive to send young offenders abroad, but it costs double to keep them locked up in a cell.

Most young offenders do not re-offend within three years of this 'therapy'. By contrast, someone who is sent to prison is more likely to commit another offence in the future.

3 What do you think of the 'therapy'?

1 Is there anything similar in your country?
2 How successful do you think it would be/has been?

4 Read the four cases on the right. Which of these punishments below would you give to each person?

PUNISHMENTS

Community service: This is where someone does something useful in the community, e.g. helps in an old people's home or does gardening in a local park.

Prison: 6 months to 5 years. (Or you can ask for the case to go to a higher court where a longer prison sentence, up to a life sentence, can be given.)

Probation: The offender has to report to a probation officer each week.

Rehabilitation: Special treatment in a centre run by social workers – home or abroad.

RUPERT LEVERETT (49) is a financier who cheated investors out of £23 million.

Lots of people have lost their life savings. Leverett transferred his money to his wife before he was arrested so this money cannot be used to provide his victims with compensation.

RAYMOND MILLIGAN (39) and CAMPBELL MORTIMER (44) were arrested for a 'vigilante' attack on a fourteen year old in their village.

The youth has committed many robberies since he moved to the village two years ago. Police cannot control the boy, who is too young to go to prison. The men locked him in a garage for two nights and terrified him by throwing 'petrol' on him. (The 'petrol' was in fact water.) Local people consider the men to be heroes.

ANITA BUCKNER (19) has been caught shoplifting several times already.

Her parents divorced when she was thirteen. Psychiatrists say she *wants* to get caught. Local shopkeepers are furious because Anita always escapes with a small fine or a warning.

TAG BAMFORD (15) paints graffiti on trains and bus stations.

He has caused damage estimated at £23,000. Local people are afraid that if the courts do not make an example of him, more and more young people will become involved in this kind of vandalism.

Focus

TOPIC
• Flight attendant training

GRAMMAR
• *Should, ought to*
• *Should have, ought to have*

FUNCTIONS
• Greetings
• Making offers

SKILLS
• Listening: a monologue
• Speaking: making and dealing with complaints

SPEECH PATTERNS
• Stress
• Contractions

The American Way to America.

American Airlines

Come fly with me!

GETTING STARTED

1 **Look at the airline advertisement and answer these questions.**

1 How are American Airlines trying to attract customers?
2 What 'image' is the advertisement trying to create?
3 Advertisements always present being a flight attendant as an attractive and exciting job. What do you think the reality is? What qualities do you think they need to do the job well?

🖻 Documentary

LISTENING

2 **Michael Killingsworth is in charge of training flight attendants for American Airlines. Before you listen to the first part of the interview with him, discuss these questions.**

1 How long do you think the training lasts?
2 What do you think the training includes?

3 🖾 **Listen and answer these questions.**

1 How long is the training programme?
2 Which of these things does Michael specifically mention as being part of the course?
   a) first aid
   b) emergency procedures
   c) uniform care
   d) customer service

4 🔊 **Listen to part of the training programme.**

1 Complete these details:

> Destination: *Seattle*   Duration: . . . . .
> Altitude: . . . . .   Weather: . . . . .

2 What else is mentioned?

3 Look at this safety announcement.

> ❝ Now we would like to direct your attention to the video screens located throughout the aircraft for a brief message about our safety features on our 767. ❞

This is an example of formal language. How would you give the same instruction to a group of friends?

5 🔊 **Michael describes the qualities flight attendants should have. Answer the questions.**

1 Which attributes does he mention as important?
  a) good looks   f) a sunny smile
  b) flexibility   g) a good sense of humour
  c) good health   h) being polite
  d) self-control   i) poise (self-assurance)
  e) personality

2 How good does he think the training is?

6 🔊 **Now listen to Michael talking about the importance of customer service.**

1 Which of the following are not given as examples of appropriate greetings? When might you use them?
  a) Hi! How are you doing?
  b) Good afternoon./Good evening.
  c) Good afternoon, ladies and gentlemen.
  d) Welcome aboard.

2 According to Michael, what is the effect of the following body language?

3 What must flight attendants remember when they serve their passengers?

4 What examples does Michael give of suitable ways of making offers?

5 After the meal has been served the attendant moves round the aircraft and speaks to passengers. Why does Michael call this 'the phase that pays'?

6 At the end of the flight what suitable expressions of leavetaking does Michael give?

DISCOVERING LANGUAGE

7 Study the two situations and answer the questions below.

A INSTRUCTOR: OK, everyone. Tomorrow is your final test, so you *should* try to have a good night's sleep.

B INSTRUCTOR: Those passengers are in the wrong seats. Did you check their boarding cards?
  TRAINEE: Sorry, I forgot.
  INSTRUCTOR: Well you know you *should have* done that.

1 Which situation gives an example of advice and which of criticism?

2 Which situation refers to the past?

3 Which word follows *should* when we move from the present to the past?

4 *Ought to* has the same meaning as *should*. Rephrase situations A and B using *ought to*.

SPEECH PATTERNS

8 🔊 **Listen to these sentences. Which words in *italics* are stressed and which are contracted?**

1 We *should have taken* a taxi. We *should not have taken* the bus.

2 They *ought to have been* more polite. They *ought not to have been* so rude.

Listen again and repeat the sentences.

SPEAKING

9 Someone from a charter airline is dealing with complaints from a dissatisfied customer.

Student B: You are the airline representative. Turn to page 128 to prepare your replies.

Student A: You have just flown back to your country after an unsatisfactory flight with a small charter airline. Make your complaints to the airline representative. You are unhappy because:

• your flight was delayed by three hours and the airline gave no information to passengers.

• you wanted a vegetarian meal (but you didn't order one); you were given a meal with meat.

• the cabin service was very poor even for a charter flight.

• they put you in a smoking seat when you wanted non-smoking.

• the airline has lost your suitcase (but you didn't put a label with your name and address on it).

• you want some kind of compensation!

Man's best friend?

Focus

TOPIC
• Guide dog training

GRAMMAR
• Tag questions
• Negative questions

SKILLS
• Speaking: a discussion
• Reading: an article
• Listening: an interview
• Writing: questions

SPEECH PATTERNS
• Intonation of tag questions

VOCABULARY DEVELOPMENT
• Making nouns from adjectives

GETTING STARTED

1 Look at the pictures and answer the questions.

1 What is the relationship between the people and the dogs in the pictures?
2 Which animals perform a useful function? How difficult would it be to train them?
3 How possible is it for a dog to really be 'one of the family'?
4 Are dogs domestic animals in your country or are they used for work?

READING

2 Read the text about guide dogs and select the best opening sentence from a)–e), for each paragraph.

a) Nevertheless, good breeding is just the beginning.
b) Seven to nine months after arriving at the training centre, a guide dog is ready to be introduced to its new owner.
c) Blind people usually spend up to four tough weeks learning how to work safely with their new guides.
d) Training has become more sophisticated over the years.
e) The first guide dogs for the blind were trained in Germany in 1916, to lead blinded ex-servicemen.

A pair of eyes

1 Guide dog training was further developed in the US and now schools which train such dogs exist in several countries. Guide dog training started in Britain in 1931 and there are around 4,000 guide dogs in Britain which help their blind and partially-sighted owners.

2 This is just as well as there used to be an eighty per cent failure rate among potential guide dogs in the early days. However, we need to realise that a guide dog is more than the product of just special training. Nowadays a breeding programme ensures the suitability of the supply of dogs which have the right physical and temperamental qualities. A good guide dog needs sensitivity, adaptability, good voice response, some initiative and a willingness to please. Crosses between labradors and golden retrievers account for around half the dogs. Pure labradors account for roughly a third while German shepherds and pure golden retrievers each contribute ten per cent.

3 Most people are unaware of the long training process. When they are about six weeks old the puppies go to live with volunteer families and are taught to be clean and obey the basic commands like 'sit', 'stay', 'down' and 'come'. They visit busy places and learn to conquer their fear of loud noises, roadworks and busy crowds, and to control their natural liveliness. By the end of their nine or ten-month stay they have acquired the three Cs – confidence, concentration and calmness – and are ready to start their training at one of the seven centres.

3 Read the three paragraphs again. Find evidence to show that these statements are true.

1 War probably led to the first training of guide dogs.
2 In Britain, the training of guide dogs has improved.
3 Mixed breeds make the best guide dogs.
4 Early training is extremely important.
5 Dogs have to grow up very quickly.

DEVELOPING VOCABULARY

4 Find the noun forms of these adjectives in the text.

suitable   sensitive   adaptable   willing   lively   confident   calm

📟 **How, if at all, does the stress change between each adjective and the noun? Use your dictionary, then listen to check.**

• suitable   •suitability

LISTENING

5 📟 Listen to the interview with Maureen O'Brian about training guide dogs and answer the questions below.

1 Which three skills does a dog first learn when it gets to the centre?
2 Why does a dog have to learn to think for itself?
3 How are dogs matched with owners?
4 What happens when the owner goes to the centre?
5 What should people never do if they want to help a blind person with a guide dog?

REVIEWING LANGUAGE

6 Look at this question from the interview.
'You have to be a psychologist, **don't you?**'
What is the purpose of the tag at the end?
What happens to the question tag if the sentence is negative?
'You don't have to be a psychologist, **do you?**'

Are these statements about question tags true or false? Correct the false statements.
1 If the sentence is positive, the tag is usually positive.
2 The tag always uses a modal or an auxiliary verb.
3 The tag depends on what is really true, *not* what the speaker thinks.

7 Complete each sentence with a question tag.

1 It's a lively dog, ... ?
2 A guide dog has to learn to think, ... ?
3 He . . . . . have the dog for long, ... ?
4 She should have checked, ... ?
5 It won't bite, ... ?

DISCOVERING LANGUAGE

8 Look at these negative questions from the interview. How would you form a positive question for A and B?

A '*Doesn't* this cause problems?'
B '*Don't you just deliver it to the new owner?*'

📟 **Now listen to the examples. What kind of answer does the speaker expect?**

9 Write negative questions for these answers.

As a matter of fact, not all dogs can be trained.
Can't all dogs be trained?

1 Yes, I have been here before, quite a lot.
2 Oh yes, I'd love to go to Thailand.
3 No, actually, we're not twins.
4 Yes, of course we should get there on time.

SPEECH PATTERNS

10 📟 Listen to four questions and answer the questions below.

1 Which kind of question do you hear in each case: positive, negative or a question tag?
2 Does the voice rise or fall at the end of each question?
3 In which questions does the person asking the questions expect a certain answer?
4 Which question genuinely asks for information?

Listen again and repeat.

11 Work in pairs. Write questions to ask your partner about things in the list below. Vary the kind of question according to whether you are checking information or asking for information.

home   family   job/studies   hobbies   ambitions   holidays

Now ask your partner.

Levels of formality

Focus

TOPIC
• Restaurant service

FUNCTIONS
• Expressing regrets
• Apologising

SKILLS
• Listening: a conversation
• Reading: letters
• Speaking: leaving a short message/ role play
• Writing: a letter of apology

STYLE
• Informal and formal expressions

☞ COMPARING CULTURES

1 Work in pairs. Discuss the following.

In the USA customers expect waiters and shop assistants to be friendly and smiling. Many British people might find this 'too much', i.e. that they are too friendly. What is appropriate in your culture?

LISTENING

2 🖭 Chloe Hawthorne runs two successful restaurants. She is talking to a waiter, Max. Listen and answer these questions.

1 What kind of person is Max?
2 How interested is he in what Chloe has to say?

Now listen again and complete the chart.

	CAFÉ CHLOE	LE JARDIN
Age of clients:	.....	.....
Type:	.....	.....
Booking:	.....	.....
Food:	.....	.....
Music:	.....	.....
Prices:	.....	.....
Waiters' behaviour:	.....	.....

READING

3 Read the letter Chloe received on Monday morning when she went to open the restaurant. Answer the questions.

1 How many complaints does Mr Metcalf have ?
2 What sort of person is Mr Metcalf?
3 Which areas of complaint had Chloe already warned Max about?
4 How do you think the letter makes Chloe feel?

The Grange
15 Lamb's Mews
London
SW19 1PF

19th January

Dear Ms Hawthorne,
I am writing to express my disappointment with the evening my wife and I spent at your restaurant two nights ago. While the food was, as usual, very good, I regret to inform you that the service from our waiter, Max, was most unsatisfactory.

First of all, when we arrived, we discovered our table overlooking the garden had been allocated to some other customers. The new table we eventually received was by the door and when I complained Max just laughed.

Furthermore, as we were sitting down, he was extremely familiar with my wife, which deeply embarrassed her. When our meal came, he served the food casually and at the end cleared the plates in a most disgusting fashion.

Regarding the payment of service, I quote your menu which states that the matter of rewarding service is at the discretion of the client. In addition, I should point out that on other occasions I have left at least 12 per cent. This time, I felt justified in leaving nothing.

I regret having to write this letter, but as a regular customer I am extremely displeased and did not expect to be treated in this manner. I look forward to hearing from you with a satisfactory reply, or, if you prefer, we could meet in person to resolve this matter.
Yours sincerely,

Rupert Metcalf.

Rupert Metcalf

SPEAKING

4 Work in pairs.

Chloe leaves a message on Max's answering machine. Decide what she says. What do you think she accuses him of doing/not doing? Begin the message:

'Max, this is Chloe. I could murder you. I have just had an awful letter from one of my best customers, Mr Metcalf ...'

READING

5 Put the parts of Max's letter to Chloe in the correct order.

Dear Chloe,

a) OK. I admit I forgot to clear the table the way I was supposed to. But by this time I was fed up with Mr Metcalf.

b) Just a short note in reply to your message on my answering machine. I'm really upset that you're so angry without even listening to my side of the story.

c) Another thing, this business about his wife, I only complimented her on her dress. *She* didn't seem to mind.

d) To start with, when Mr and Mrs Metcalf finally turned up they were at least 45 minutes late. That's why I had given their table to some other customers.

e) He is notoriously mean and according to the other staff always leaves tiny tips.

f) I am really sorry that I have had to write this letter. I can understand that you're angry, but I'm really upset too. I apologise if I have caused you problems, but I've been really popular at the 'Café'. Let's talk and sort things out. Hope to hear from you soon.

g) As far as service goes, I know it says service is up to the client, but I think he just uses it as an excuse to leave little or nothing.

h) As for the other table by the door, I went to a lot of trouble to set it up. When he moaned about where it was, I couldn't help laughing.

All the best,

Max

6 What really happened between Rupert Metcalf and Max in the restaurant? Whose side of the story do you believe?

FOCUS ON STYLE

7 Make a list of any formal and informal expressions in the two letters.

1 Find two ways of saying the same thing.
I am writing to . . . /Just a short note to . . .
complain/moan, arrive/turn up

2 Match Rupert Metcalf's statements with Max's statements.

FOCUS ON FUNCTIONS

8 Find ways of apologising and expressing regrets in the two letters.

SPEAKING

9 Work in pairs.

Student A: You are Max.

Student B: You are Chloe. You meet to discuss what happened at 'Le Jardin'.

1 Try to establish the facts.
2 Arrive at a solution that is fair to Max and good for Chloe's business.

WRITING

10 Write Chloe's reply to Mr Metcalf. Begin:

Dear Mr Metcalf,
I am writing to apologise for what happened the other evening at 'Le Jardin'.

Follow this format. Remember to make the letter fairly formal.

• Respond to his complaints and give explanations for the table and Max's style of service.
• Tell him what action you have decided to take about Max.
• Offer some kind of compensation to Mr Metcalf. Say you hope he will accept it.

Finish like this:

Once again, I hope you will accept my most sincere apologies for what happened the other evening. I can assure you that it will not happen again. We look forward to seeing you again at 'Le Jardin'.
Yours sincerely

Grammar reference

1 *Should* and *ought to*

- The modal verb *should* is often used for giving advice. The speaker thinks that something is a good idea, and is expressing a personal opinion.
  EXAMPLE: *If you're going for an interview, you **should** wear a suit and have a hair cut.* (Notice that you only have to use *should* once.)

- *Should(n't)* can also be used to say that you think something is morally right.
  EXAMPLES: *People **shouldn't** drive so fast.*
  *Prisons **should** reform people, not just punish them.*

- *Ought* means the same as *should*, and is followed by the infinitive with *to*.
  EXAMPLE: *He **ought** to wear a suit to the interview.*
  Sometimes *ought* is stronger than *should* and expresses an idea of obligation or duty.
  EXAMPLE: *You **ought** to write to your mother more often.*

2 *Should have* and *ought to have*

- Sentences with *should(n't) have* are used to criticise what someone did or didn't do in the past.
  EXAMPLES: *We **should have** set off for the airport earlier.*
  *So you didn't get the job? Well, you **shouldn't have** worn jeans to the interview.*

- *Ought to have* has the same meaning.
  EXAMPLE: *You **ought to have** worn a suit.*

FORM

- *Should have* and *ought to have* are followed by a past participle. Notice the question form: *Should I have worn a suit?* Questions beginning with *Ought* (*Ought I to have said something?*) are uncommon.

- The negative form *ought not to have* (*oughtn't to have*) is less common than *shouldn't have*.

3 Question tags

- We usually use a negative question tag with a positive statement: *You speak French, **don't you**?* and a positive question tag with a negative statement: *You haven't been here before, **have you**?*
  The tense of the question tag is the same as the tense of the statement.

- The question tag uses either an auxiliary verb (as in the examples above), a modal verb:
  *You will come to the airport, **won't you**?*
  or the verb *to be*:
  *We're late, **aren't we**?*

Be careful to use the correct auxiliary or modal after a contraction.
  EXAMPLES: *She'd never been to Greece before, **had she**?* (She had never . . .)
  *You'd rather watch TV, **wouldn't you**?* (You would rather . . .)

- The question tag after *Let's* is *shall we*?
  EXAMPLE: *Let's go out for dinner tonight, **shall we**?*

- After either a positive or a negative imperative the question tag is *will you*?
  EXAMPLES: *Sit down, **will you**?*
  *Please don't be late, **will you**?*
  If an offer is made, *won't you* is used.
  EXAMPLE: *Take a seat, **won't you**?*

- The intonation of a question tag is important. Rising intonation usually means you are asking a real question – you want to know the answer. Falling intonation means you expect the other person to agree with you – you know what answer you expect.

- Be careful how you answer a question tag after a negative statement.
  EXAMPLE:

| *You can't swim, can you?* | *Yes.* (= I can swim.) |
| | *No.* (= I can't swim.) |

4 Negative questions

- A question without a negative (*not*) is neutral – the speaker doesn't know the answer.
  EXAMPLE: *Are you hungry?*
  The speaker of a negative question expects or hopes for the answer *Yes*.
  EXAMPLE: *Aren't you hungry?* (You didn't have any breakfast.)

- A negative question can express surprise (as in the example above), anxiety, disapproval or persuasion.
  EXAMPLES: ***Don't** you love me any more?*
  ***Can't** you remember anything I tell you?*
  ***Won't** you stay for five minutes?*

- Notice how the word *not* comes immediately after the verb.

FORM

- Negative questions are usually contracted, with the word *not* coming immediately afer the verb *to be*, the auxiliary or the modal verb, and before the subject, as in the above examples.

Progress check Units 2–3

GRAMMAR AND FUNCTIONS

1 What would you say in these situations? Use *must* or *have to* in each sentence.

1 You are the caretaker of a building. Someone asks you to describe your duties.
2 You see some children who are about to go skating on a frozen pond. You know that it is much more dangerous than it looks.
3 You and your friend are going to a concert which starts one hour from now. The journey there will only take fifteen minutes.

2 Rewrite each sentence without changing its meaning. Begin with the words you are given.

1 Wayne was made to clean the kitchen floor.
Martha made Wayne …
2 The government doesn't let people under seventeen drive.
People under seventeen …
3 The teachers ask us not to wear make-up, but lots of girls do.
We …
4 His parents don't mind him playing the drums at home.
His parents …

3 What would you say to your friend in these situations? Use a negative question each time.

Your friend is carrying a book that you think is yours.
Isn't that my book?

1 Your friend doesn't want to come to a pop concert with you.
2 You didn't see your friend at school yesterday.
3 You want your friend to come in for a cup of coffee.
4 You think the girl across the road is your friend's sister.
5 You are impatiently waiting for your friend to finish writing a composition.

4 Match the beginnings of these sentences with the best endings to make six complete sentences.

1 I think you ought to
2 We should have
3 Small children should be
4 They shouldn't have
5 You shouldn't be
6 You ought not to

a) swim immediately after you've eaten.
b) so impatient next time.
c) promised to help us if they were too busy.
d) complained to the manager.
e) apologise to your mother immediately.
f) taught how to cross the road safely.

5 Complete the text with these words or phrases.

and   despite   although   but
despite the fact that

[1]….. I couldn't really afford it, I had decided to fly to Ireland instead of going by boat. Eileen met me at Cork [2]….. it was only a short drive from there to Dungarvan. [3]….. the rain which started as soon as we left the airport, the green, gently-rolling landscape looked beautiful. I felt tired after the journey, [4]….. I wanted to explore the town. People seemed so friendly and relaxed. I soon realised that [5]….. Ireland is so close to England, it has a very different culture.

VOCABULARY

6 Match a word from column A with a word from column B to make eight compound nouns. Use each word once only.

1 ski
2 state
3 school
4 guide
5 shop
6 final
7 flight
8 cabin

a) attendant
b) assistant
c) crew
d) instructor
e) school
f) uniform
g) examination
h) dog

Well-travelled

Things that shape us

Focus

TOPIC
• Nomadic cultures

GRAMMAR
• Superlative + present perfect
• Comparisons using *the ... , the ...*

FUNCTIONS
• Cause and effect

SKILLS
• Reading: a magazine article
• Writing: a description

VOCABULARY DEVELOPMENT
• Words relating to geography, climate, character, natural disasters

GETTING STARTED

1 Look at the pictures and match the people with the part of the world they inhabit.

READING

2 Read the article about nomads and answer these questions.

1 What do different nomadic groups have in common?
2 Why do you think the writer admires them?

Noble nomads

Nomadic societies around the world have much in common. Whether looking for pasture with flocks of sheep or herds of reindeer, or like the Sioux, who once followed bison across the plains of North America, they are all governed by the imperative to move on. Because of this need for mobility, individuals in nomadic societies share most of their belongings.

They most often live in small groups or tribes because the land cannot support large numbers. The size of the tribe will depend on what nature is able to provide. In very hostile environments, the smaller the group, the easier it is to survive. Their isolation means they have to be self-sufficient and as a result they can be introverted and suspicious of strangers. Strict moral codes govern the members of nomadic societies and their treatment of travellers. The fiercest Tuareg warrior can be the most wonderful host. The best hospitality I have ever received was in a tent in the middle of the Sahara desert.

Nomads are less greedy than 'civilised' man. Owing to their reliance on nature, they live in balance with it, only harvesting enough to satisfy their needs. Consequently, they are unable to understand civilised invaders who plunder the land and animal life and threaten their existence. That is why they fight back and, due to their treatment of settlers, they have been labelled 'savages'.

No one is tougher than the nomad who can endure a level of pain and discomfort which people in the so-called civilised world would find intolerable. That is why boys in many such societies undergo severe initiations, to prove they are truly ready for the tests of manhood. In the face of disaster they appear fatalistic; ready to accept anything that nature can throw at them. Despite drought, famine and other hardships they fight to survive, although history shows us that the struggle is usually unsuccessful. ■

FOCUS ON FUNCTIONS

3 Find words in the article which express consequences and results.

4 Rewrite these sentences using the form given in brackets.

They had to move on because the sheep ate all the grass. (consequently)
The sheep ate all the grass. Consequently, they had to move on.

1 They died out because the climate changed. (owing to)
2 They live on reservations because their land was taken from them. (that is why)
3 After the destruction of the bison many starved. (due to)
4 They were called savages because they killed the settlers. (as a result)
5 White men came and made them leave their lands. (because of)
6 They fight to survive because drought and famine are common. (consequently)

REVIEWING LANGUAGE

5 Look at this sentence from the article.

The best hospitality I have ever received was in a tent in the middle of the Sahara desert.

1 Is the person describing a general fact or a personal experience?
2 Is the person still in the tent in the desert?
3 Which tense follows the superlative?

6 Use the prompts to make similar sentences.

1 they/tall people/I ever see/live/tiny huts
2 boring talk/I ever listen to/about parrots
3 bad meal/she ever eat/in England
4 less interesting man/I ever meet/talk for hours non-stop

7 Work in pairs. Talk about the time you felt:
coldest   saddest   angriest   most frightened

DISCOVERING LANGUAGE

8 Look at this sentence from the article.

The smaller the group, the easier it is to survive.

Does the sentence express a comparison or a consequence?

9 Use the prompts to make similar sentences.
cold/weather   depressed/population/be
The colder the weather, the more depressed the population is.

1 hot /temperature   lazy/people/be
2 rich/people   difficult/they/be
3 difficult/job   hard/I/try
4 difficult/journey   more satisfying/be

Now make generalisations about your own country.

In England, the further south you go, the less friendly people are.

DEVELOPING VOCABULARY

10 Study the words below and list them under these headings.

GEOGRAPHY	DISASTERS	CLIMATE	CHARACTER

earthquake   excitable   introverted   waterfall
talkative   lake   frost   calm   freezing
easy-going   damp   fatalistic   desert   glacier
arid   optimistic   mountainous   avalanche
storm   flood   mist   ice   drought   pessimistic
passive   jungle   forest

Which words do you associate with these types of country?
Type A: dark, wet, cold countries, e.g. Sweden.
Type B: dry, sunny countries, e.g. Mexico.
Type C: warm and humid countries, e.g. Thailand.

WRITING

11 Work in pairs.

Imagine you want to tell a foreigner about how you think geography and climate have affected the character of your country. Use some of the ways of expressing consequences and results you looked at in Exercise 5. Think of these areas:

a) dress   e) behaviour and customs
b) occupations   f) attitudes
c) daily routines   g) wealth
d) free time

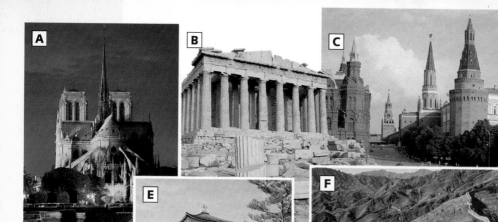

Focus

TOPIC
- Tourism

GRAMMAR
- Definite, indefinite and zero article

SKILLS
- Listening: a literary extract
- Reading: a literary extract
- Speaking: a discussion

Paradise lost?

GETTING STARTED

1 How many of these sights can you identify?

2 Are *you* a culture vulture? Look at the statements below and give them a score out of five.

5 = completely agree → 0 = totally disagree

1   Visiting historic places and viewing great works of art makes us better people.
2   I'd rather spend time in a gallery than on a beach.
3   Whenever I travel I always make sure I visit the most important sights.
4   Before I travel I always try to find something out about the history of the place I am visiting.
5   I would rather watch a folk dancing display than shop for cheap bargains.

LISTENING

3 You are going to listen to an extract from the novel *Paradise News* by David Lodge. One of its main characters is an expert on tourism called Sheldrake. Before you listen, guess the answer to these questions.

1   How many people a minute do you think enter Notre Dame Cathedral in Paris?
   a) 80   b) 108   c) 118   d) 180
2   The risks of getting an infection if you swim in the Mediterranean are one in:
   a) 6   b) 10   c) 20   d) 50
3   How many raft trips down the Colorado River are there each day?
   a) 10   b) 100   c) 500   d) 1,000
4   How many million international travellers could there be by the year 2000?
   a) 500   b) 650   c) 1,000   d) 1,500

4 Now listen and check if you were right.

5 Listen again and complete the chart.

PLACE	DETAIL	PROBLEM	CAUSE
Lake District	*footpaths*	*have become trenches*	*too many walkers*
Sistine Chapel	.....	*being damaged*	*breath and body heat*
Notre Dame	*stonework*	.....	*exhaust fumes*
Alpine resorts	.....	.....	.....

REVIEWING LANGUAGE

6 Look at these rules about the use of articles.

A We do not usually use articles before:
   a) plural countable nouns used in a non-specific way.
   b) abstract nouns.
   c) names of countries (with some exceptions; see Grammar reference page 38).
B We use the indefinite article (*a*) when we are referring to a singular countable noun in a non-specific way.
C We use the definite article (*the*):
   a) when we refer to something specific.
   b) when we mention something for the second time.
   c) when there is only one of something.
   d) when the object or place is known to everybody.
   e) in superlative constructions.
   f) with some titles and place names.

Find evidence for the rules in these sentences.

1 Many countries have *a district with lakes*.
2 *The Lake District* has footpaths.
3 *The footpaths* in the Lake District have become trenches.
4 Where is *the guidebook*? It's in *the bedroom*.
5 We went along *a footpath; the footpath* had become like a trench.
6 *Italy* is full of *frescoes*.
7 *The frescoes* in *the Sistine Chapel* are being destroyed.
8 They are *the most beautiful frescoes* in *the world*.
9 *Beauty* can bring its own problems.
10 *The beauty* of these lakes is breathtaking.

7 Complete the sentences using *a, the* or Ø (no article).

One day on holiday last year ¹..... weather was awful so we decided to go on ²..... trip to Roker Castle in ³..... south-east of England. I had last visited ⁴..... castle when I was ⁵..... child and I had ⁶..... happy memories of it. I planned ⁷..... trip in detail. Unfortunately ⁸..... castle had completely changed. There were hundreds of ⁹..... tourists and ¹⁰..... really cheap souvenir shop which changed ¹¹..... atmosphere. You can imagine ¹²..... disappointment I felt, one of ¹³..... best memories of my childhood had been destroyed.

READING

8 In this extract from *Paradise News*, Sheldrake explains why he started to study tourism. Read and find out his theory about it. Do you agree?

I always hated holidays, even as a kid. Such a waste of time, sitting on the beach, making sandpies, when you could be at home doing some interesting hobby. Then, when I got engaged, we were both students at the time, my fiancée insisted on dragging me off to Europe to see the sights: Paris, Venice, Florence, the usual things. Bored the pants off me, till one day, sitting on a lump of rock beside the Parthenon, watching the tourists milling about, clicking their cameras, talking to each other in umpteen different languages, it suddenly struck me: tourism is the new world religion. Catholics, Protestants, Hindus, Muslims, Buddhists, atheists – the only thing they have in common is they all believe in the importance of seeing the Parthenon. Or the Sistine Chapel, or the Eiffel Tower.

9 Find words and expressions which mean:

1 felt extremely uninterested.
2 a piece.
3 moving around with no real purpose.
4 a lot (informal).

10 Find evidence in the extract to show that these statements are true.

1 Sheldrake didn't like holidays as a child.
2 He was an unenthusiastic tourist.
3 He had a poor opinion of tourists.

SPEAKING

11 Work in groups and discuss these questions.

1 Is tourism a waste of everybody's time?
2 What would happen if everybody stayed at home instead of travelling?
3 Can you think of places in your own country which have been destroyed by tourism?
4 What could be done to rescue them?
5 How could people be educated to be good tourists?

A sense of the dramatic

Focus

TOPIC
• Travel
• Explorations

SKILLS
• Listening: a monologue
• Speaking: describing a dramatic event

STYLE
• Sentence length
• Creating suspense

VOCABULARY DEVELOPMENT
• Words creating a dramatic effect

SPEECH PATTERNS
• Creating a dramatic effect: stress

GETTING STARTED

1 Study this usage note.

> 17
>
> USAGE
> Compare **travel(s)**, **journey**, **voyage** and **trip**.
>
> The general activity of moving from one place to another is **travel**:
> - *He came home after years of foreign travel.*
>
> If a person moves from place to place over a period of years we speak of their **travels**:
> - *Did you go to Rome during your travels?*
>
> A **journey** is the time spent and the distance covered in going from one particular place to another:
> - *It is a long journey by train from Paris to Moscow.*
> - *Persepolis was ten days' journey across the desert.*
>
> A **voyage** has the same meaning but it is only by sea:
> - *The voyage from England to Australia used to take several months.*
>
> A **trip** is a short journey, or one on which you only spend a short time in another place, then come back:
> - *We'll have time for a trip to France next weekend.*

Now complete these sentences with a suitable word.

1 We're going on a short ..... to Venice.
2 In the old days, the sea ..... to Australia from England took months.
3 I haven't seen you for ages, have you been on your ..... again?
4 The explorers made their ..... overland by camel.

🎧 Documentary

LISTENING

2 📼 Matt Dickinson talks about his career as an explorer and contrasts two dangerous experiences. Listen and answer the questions. The first experience took place in the Namib Desert.

1 How far has Matt Dickinson travelled since 1976?
2 Where is the Namib Desert?
3 How long did the journey take?
4 What equipment and supplies did they take?
5 What was their daily routine?
6 Why did he find walking through the forest a strange experience?

3 📼 Now listen to Matt talking about his experience on the Brahmaputra River and answer the questions.

1 What is the Brahmaputra River like?
2 What was the cause of the accident?
3 How does Dickinson compare the dangers of the desert and the Brahmaputra experience?
4 What do you think he means when he talks about the 'different approaches mentally and physically' he needed for these two different experiences?

4 Work in pairs. Discuss these questions.

1 What do you think of Matt Dickinson's 'career'?
2 What do you think motivates him?
3 Are his travels of any value to other people?

SPEECH PATTERNS

6 🔊 **Listen to the extract again and decide which words are strongly stressed.**

FOCUS ON STYLE

7 Another way that Matt creates a sense of drama is through sentence length.

Most of the sentences in the extract are long and quite complex. What effect does the sentence 'Well it did.' have on the dramatic impact of the passage?

8 Matt also uses the technique of suspense. He seems to leave us at the point where we don't know what happens next.

*'Then it was the **horrifying** experience of being **swept** completely out of control, with our raft upside down, down the Brahmaputra to we knew not what fate.'*

What do you think happened next?

SPEAKING

9 Work in pairs.

Decide how to impress your partner by making your text below more dramatic. Choose your vocabulary carefully and vary the sentence length. When you tell your story make sure you make it *sound* dramatic and exciting.

Student A: ❝ I was in the desert in a land rover when there was a sandstorm. The storm blew the land rover over and we jumped out. The sand went in my eyes and mouth, in fact it went everywhere. It was difficult to breathe. I thought I was going to suffocate (die because I had no air to breathe). I wrapped a scarf around my head. The storm finally stopped after twelve hours and we were rescued by some Tuaregs. ❞

Student B: ❝ I was in a small plane. Suddenly we hit a storm and the plane was shaken about for about five minutes. Everybody was frightened and screaming except for me. The pilot said he was out of control. The engine stopped and we started to dive (go down fast). Luckily the engine started and the pilot managed to land safely at the airport. ❞

10 Think of something dramatic or exciting which happened to you. Tell your story, making it dramatic. Think about:

- your choice of vocabulary
- sentence length
- suspense

DEVELOPING VOCABULARY

5 Look at how Matt creates a sense of drama.

Matt Dickinson has obviously told the story about falling into the Brahmaputra many times. He creates a sense of drama by his choice of vocabulary. Matt chooses his words carefully to give us the sensation of what falling into the river was really like.

Read the transcript of what he says. Which of the words in bold type means:

a) to breathe quickly, and noisily, with difficulty?
b) very frightening?
c) to move with twisting turns?
d) to move quickly up and down, as on water?
e) very cold?
f) to be moved quickly and powerfully?
g) to push suddenly and violently into water?
h) a sudden rapid movement?

❝ Now, we were extremely lucky on several occasions to avoid being tipped out of the boat, but we all knew that eventually disaster might strike. And it was only a matter of time, as we **bobbed** our way down the river, often out of control, that some mishap would occur. Well it did. We went into a wave which was far too big for our rubber raft to survive and I felt the extreme **rush** of adrenalin as the **freezing** cold water bit into us and I was **plunged** into the water, as the boat went over. I felt the air being sucked out of my lungs and as I came out of the **swirling** white water into which we'd been plunged, I was **gasping** for breath and completely disorientated. And then it was the **horrifying** experience of being **swept** completely out of control, with our raft upside down, down the Brahmaputra River to we knew not what fate. ❞

Grammar reference

1 Making superlative comparisons

- Superlatives are often followed by the present perfect or past perfect tenses, and the word *ever*.
  EXAMPLES: *This is the most interesting city I have (ever) visited.*
  It was the best holiday I had ever had.
  We could also say: *I have never visited such an interesting city (before).* The perfect tense is used because we mean 'in my life up to now/then'.

- Notice that we say:
  the biggest city in the world
  the hottest place on (the) earth
  the happiest day of my life.

2 The more ... the more ...

- We sometimes use the comparative form of an adjective or adverb, or the word *more* on its own, when we want to show that there is a logical relationship between things.
  EXAMPLES: *The faster we went, the more frightened I felt.*
  The more (money) she earned, the more (money) she spent.
  The more expensive the hotel (is), the better the facilities (are).
  Notice how the verb *to be* can be omitted from one or both parts of this kind of sentence.

3 The indefinite article

- We use the indefinite article (*a / an*) when we are referring to a singular countable noun for the first time, or when we are not specifying which one we mean.
  EXAMPLE: *A man was waiting outside the house.*

4 The definite article

We use the definite article (*the*):

- when something becomes definite or specific because we are mentioning it again, or because we add extra information.
  EXAMPLES: *The man waiting outside the house was dressed in black.*
  Where are the photographs I showed you yesterday?

- when everyone knows which one we mean.
  EXAMPLES: *Amanda is in the garden.* (our garden)
  Where's the dog? (our dog)
  I'm staying at the Bell Hotel. (the one in this town)
  The Queen is visiting Birmingham tomorrow.

- when there is only one of something.
  EXAMPLES: *the world, the moon, the Parthenon.*

- with adjectives referring to classes or categories of people, including nationalities when we are considering them as a group.
  EXAMPLES: *the rich, the unemployed, the disabled, the English, the Germans.*

- for a whole species.
  EXAMPLE: *The white rhino is in danger of extinction.*

- with the names of most rivers, seas, oceans, mountain ranges, geographical regions, groups of islands, and plural names of countries.
  EXAMPLES: *the Amazon, the Atlantic, the Alps, the Gobi Desert, the Middle East, the Seychelles.*

- when we talk about playing a musical instrument.
  EXAMPLE: *She plays the violin very well.*

- to refer to some public places, when we are considering them as particular buildings.
  EXAMPLES: *I'm going to the bank/cinema/supermarket.*

5 No article

No article is used:

- with most squares, streets, towns, cities, lakes, countries and names of buildings.
  EXAMPLES: *Constitution Square, Regent Street, Lake Superior, Buckingham Palace.*

- when we are speaking generally.
  EXAMPLES: *Love has inspired many great poets.*
  I like dogs. (But: *I was terrified of the dogs on the farm.*)
  She hates cheese. (But: *We ate the cheese she had bought for lunch.*)
  Money can't buy happiness. (But: *I can't describe the happiness I felt when I saw him again.*)

FORM

- *Because of, Owing to* and *Due to* are prepositions which introduce a noun phrase.
  EXAMPLE: *Owing to the bad weather, the flight was cancelled.*
  The noun phrase (*the bad weather*) is the explanation or cause of what follows (the cancellation of the flight).
  As a result, Consequently and *That is why* are connectors. They connect the sentence they introduce with the meaning of the previous sentence.
  EXAMPLE: *The weather was bad. As a result, the flight was cancelled.*

Talkback

Entrepreneurs!

1 You are so fed up and bored with the restaurants in your town that you and your friends want to open a restaurant yourselves. You have found 200 square metres of premises in the centre of your town, but in an *unfashionable* area. Work in groups. Discuss and make decisions about the following.

1 Think of a name for the restaurant.
2 What kind of food will you serve? Write a simple menu.
3 Think of a theme for it, e.g. western, dancing, cabaret.
4 What kind of atmosphere do you want to create, e.g. bright and exciting, dark and romantic, cool and sophisticated?
5 What kind of music/entertainment will you have?
6 Which age group do you want to appeal to?
7 What will your rest day be?
8 What price range will your restaurant have? (Remember the more expensive the restaurant, the fewer clients you are likely to have!)
9 Which famous person will you invite to open the restaurant on its first evening?

2 Before you open your restaurant, you need to take these steps. The time for each step is given. Work in groups and decide the following.

a) When is the earliest that you can open it?
b) Which things could be going on at the same time?
c) Which things would it not be possible to do at the same time?

1 Apply for permission from the city council **6 weeks**
2 Advertise, interview and select waiters/waitresses **1 month**
3 Put in carpets **2 days**
4 Find a good cook **1-2 months**
5 Buy food from market **1 day**
6 Buy china, cutlery and glasses (from order to delivery) **5 weeks**
7 Write a guest list for the opening party **2 days**
8 Select and buy furniture for restaurant (you may have to order it) **6 weeks**
9 Install telephones **3 weeks**
10 Build bathrooms **5 weeks**
11 Buy plants and pictures for restaurant **3 days**
12 Order drinks **2 weeks**
13 Print and distribute invitations for opening party **2 weeks**
14 Equip kitchen **3 weeks**
15 Decorate restaurant **2 weeks**
16 Buy tablecloths and napkins **1 week**

Present your answer as a chart and compare with the other groups in your class.

COUNTDOWN	ACTION(S)
. . . . . weeks	Apply for permission from city council

5 *Just the job*

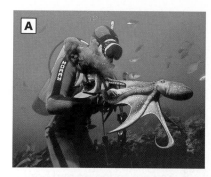

Earning a living

Focus

TOPIC
- Working conditions

GRAMMAR
- *Only if, unless, otherwise*

SKILLS
- Listening: a monologue
- Speaking: a discussion

VOCABULARY DEVELOPMENT
- Adjectives used to describe jobs

GETTING STARTED

1 Work in pairs. Discuss these questions.

1 What are the most important things for you in your present job or a future job?
2 Look at the pictures of people at work. Identify the jobs and discuss the one(s) you would like to do or would hate to do.

2 Read what the people say about their jobs. Match the descriptions with the pictures.

1 ❝Well, the money isn't that good, but it's rewarding in other ways, I mean you really feel you're doing something worthwhile – if you get someone out of a blazing building you've made a difference. It's not boring, like some other jobs. There is always something unexpected.❞

2 ❝It's an interesting life on the platform, but it's very demanding working twelve-hour days. You have to balance that against the free time. After two weeks we get a fortnight on shore.❞

3 ❝You've got to have a good head for heights and be very safety conscious – you don't get any second chances in this job. It is dangerous – but I suppose that's why it is well-paid.❞

4 ❝The job itself is awful really, you know, the dirt and noise make it stressful. The best thing about it is the other people you work with. The worst thing is in winter – you go down in the dark and come up in the dark – still, at least I've got a job, although it isn't as secure as it was.❞

5 ❝People are surprised that a woman can get to the top of this profession, but we love excitement, just like men. I think the most challenging thing is pitting your intelligence against an animal's strength.❞

6 ❝You can't stay down very long, even with a wet suit you soon get cold. It's a young man's job: I'll be out by the time I'm thirty, even though you earn a fortune.❞

DEVELOPING VOCABULARY

3 These adjectives are often used to describe jobs. Find them in the texts. What do they mean?

stressful demanding well-paid boring worthwhile
challenging secure dangerous rewarding

4 Which two adjectives from the list in Exercise 3 do you think best describe each of the following occupations?

1 civil servant   6 vet   10 supermarket cashier
2 accountant   7 nurse   11 fashion model
3 plumber   8 soldier   12 manager
4 surgeon   9 electrician 13 computer salesman
5 stockbroker

SPEAKING

5 How do you feel about your own, or your parents' jobs?

🖳 Documentary

LISTENING

6 📼 Bill McIntosh, the manager of an oil platform in the North Sea, talks about work and life on the platform. Listen and complete the timetable.

	DAY SHIFT CREW	NIGHT SHIFT CREW
Starts work	. . . . .	7.00 p.m.
Breakfast	. . . . .	. . . . .
Lunch	. . . . . a.m. – 12.30 p.m.	. . . . .
Finishes work	. . . . .	7.00 a.m.
Last meal	6.30 p.m.	6.30 a.m. – 7.30 a.m.

7 📼 Listen to Bill talking about safety regulations. Look at the pictures. Which items have to be worn if people are working outside?

helmet   boots   life jacket
goggles
life-line   coveralls

8 📼 Bill talks about work benefits.
What does he say are the benefits of the job in terms of:
1 pay?   2 time?

DISCOVERING LANGUAGE

9 Look at what Bill says.
'*Nobody can leave unless they are properly attired.*' (*attired* = dressed)

Does this mean:
a) people can leave without being properly dressed?
b) people can leave only if they are properly dressed?

Now look at the three sentences below which mean approximately the same. Which of the words in **bold** type:

a) introduces a condition?
b) introduces a consequence?
c) means *if not*?

1 Nobody can leave **unless** they are properly dressed.
2 People can leave **only if** they are properly dressed.
3 People have to be properly dressed, **otherwise** they can't leave.

10 Change these sentences, using the other two forms.

You can attend the conference only if you register.
You have to register, **otherwise** *you can't attend the conference.*
You can't attend the conference **unless** *you register.*

1 Wear a suit otherwise they won't give you the job.
2 We can wait for you if you're ready in five minutes.
3 You can't apply if you don't speak English.

SPEAKING

11 Work in pairs. Discuss these questions.

1 Do you think people on an oil platform work hard?
2 Why do they choose this job?
3 Would you work on one? Why?/Why not?

First jobs

Focus

TOPIC
- Temporary jobs

GRAMMAR
- Narrative tenses: past simple/past progressive/past perfect/past perfect progressive

SKILLS
- Reading: a narrative
- Listening: an anecdote
- Speaking: a narrative

SPEECH PATTERNS
- Adding information: intonation

GETTING STARTED

1 Work in pairs and discuss these statements.

1 Children over the age of fourteen should receive pocket money each week as a right.
2 Children should *not* expect to be paid for doing small jobs for their parents.
3 A part-time job is a good way of teaching children the value of money.

↻ COMPARING CULTURES

2 Work in pairs. Discuss these questions.

1 At what ages is it usual for people to start work in your countries?
2 How common is it for children to have part-time jobs like delivering papers or working in a family business?

READING

3 Read the story of Pat's first job and explain the cartoon.

1 Where is she?
2 What is she doing and why?

4 Now answer these questions.

1 Did Pat enjoy her job?
2 What happened with difficult customers?
3 How do we know the sale was important?
4 How do you think Pat felt when she finally got out from under the table?

My first JOB

When I was a sixth former, I got a summer job in a posh department store to finance my first trip abroad. It was near my home so it seemed ideal. The first place I worked was in the silks department. I didn't get any training so I was terrified of cutting the fabrics. There were some regular customers who came with servants and chauffeurs. Some had been coming for years. Most of them were pleasant, but a few were really nasty. Often, when somebody notorious appeared, the experienced staff ran away and hid. They only came out from the store room after the customer had gone.

> 'I'll always remember the first day of the sales.'

I'll always remember the first day of the sales. I had set my alarm early so as not to be late. I quickly dressed and left the flat. Outside, it was raining hard and the traffic was creeping along. When I got to work, people were already queuing outside the doors. Some had been waiting all night and the weather hadn't improved their temper. They were potentially a dangerous mob and I could see why our boss had planned the sale like a military operation. The previous day, my

5 Guess the meanings of these words:

1 posh   3 notorious   5 stampede
2 nasty   4 crucial   6 stuck

DISCOVERING LANGUAGE

6 Look at these three sentences from the story.

A *Some customers had been coming for years.*
B *Some had been waiting all night.*
C *I quickly dressed and left the flat.*

1 Which sentence expresses:
   a) actions taking place on several occasions up to the time of the narrative?
   b) two actions, one after the other, in the main part of the narrative?
   c) a continuous action starting before the time of the narrative, continuing up to that time?
2 Rewrite sentences A and B:
   a) as questions.   b) in the negative.

'commander' had told me to work at one of the tables in the middle of the shop floor.

At five to nine we were all waiting anxiously, as the seconds ticked by. Suddenly, the doors opened and there was the sound of hundreds of pairs of feet running through the foyer. At the crucial moment, just as the first customers were approaching, I dropped my scissors. I was crawling around under the table when the stampede struck. I was stuck underneath it for twenty minutes, surrounded by a sea of legs. I was completely helpless!

7 Use the past perfect progressive or the past simple to complete these sentences.

1 My boss ..... (work) in the company for six years when I ..... (start).
2 By 1993 I ..... (live) in Oxford for ten years.
3 I ..... (be) so bored with the job. For two years I ..... (do) the same thing every day.
4 They ..... (try) to contact me all evening, but I ..... (not arrive) home until midnight.

REVIEWING LANGUAGE

8 Look at Paragraph 2 of the story and underline all the past tenses used.

Which tense is used to express:
a) background action, often in progress when the narrative begins?
b) completed actions which form the main progression of the narrative?
c) completed actions which happened earlier than the main focus of the narrative?
d) continuous actions which started before the main focus of the narrative?

Now look at Paragraphs 1 and 3. Find at least one example of each tense described above.

9 Complete the next part of Pat's story by putting the verbs in brackets into an appropriate form.

Later on, while I [1]..... (work) in the china department, something awful [2]..... (happen). At that time I [3]..... (work) on the cash desk. On this particular occasion, it [4]..... (be) the end of the day, about 6.30 p.m. It [5]..... (be) a really busy day; the assistants [6]..... (serve) customers since 8.30 a.m. and I [7]..... (take) money continuously for ten hours.

After I [8]..... (finish) counting the money in my till I [9]..... (leave) it in a bag while I [10]..... (help) the cashier on my right count hers. When I [11]..... (turn) round I [12]..... (see) that my cash bag [13]..... (disappear) while I [14]..... (help) my colleague. By that time all the customers [15]..... (leave) the store. I [16]..... (not believe) that someone [17]..... (steal) it. I [18]..... (report) the theft to the chief cashier who [19]..... (always be) nice to me in the past, but he [20]..... (be) obviously a little suspicious of me after that day.

LISTENING

10 🔲 Listen to the description of Andy's first job and answer these questions.

1 What was the job?
2 Where was his first task and why was it dangerous?
3 How did he move along the ledge?
4 What could people see of him?

SPEECH PATTERNS

11 🔲 Listen again to the way Andy adds extra information about the belt he used.

What happens to his voice as he adds extra information?

... the only safety feature that the window cleaners had was a belt, a canvas belt with two ropes, one at each side.

Listen and repeat what he says. Then say this in a similar way.

'I've just bought a new bicycle, a shiny red bicycle, with sixteen gears, and two baskets, one at the front and one at the back.'

SPEAKING

12 Work in pairs. Now describe your first day at school or at work.

My worst job ever

FOCUS ON LITERATURE

1 Read the following.

Dickens (1812–1870) is considered one of England's most important novelists. He had a happy childhood until his father went to prison. Charles had to work in a warehouse and never forgot the misery of the experience. These adapted extracts are from *David Copperfield*, the most autobiographical of his novels.

2 Read the text quickly and decide which paragraphs deal with:

a) David's workmates.
b) David's feelings on the first day.
c) David's place of work.
d) the business David worked in.

3 Answer the questions after each paragraph.

Focus

TOPIC
• Unpleasant work

SKILLS
• Reading: literary extracts
• Writing: a narrative

STYLE
• Irony

VOCABULARY DEVELOPMENT
• Words related to *moving* and *crying*

FOCUS ON STYLE

4 Look at this definition.
Find the sentence in Paragraph 3 which contains *auspiciously*.

aus·pi·cious /ɔːˈspɪʃəs/ *adj fml* giving, promising or showing signs of future success: *an auspicious occasion* – opposite **inauspicious**- **~ly** *adv*: *The year began auspiciously with good trade figures.*

Dickens is using 'irony'. He means the opposite of what he actually says! The text tells us that his experience was sad and *inauspicious*.

PARAGRAPH 1

Murdstone and Grinby's warehouse was at the water side. Its rooms, discoloured with the dirt and smoke of a hundred years, its decaying floors and staircase; the squeaking and scratching of the old grey rats down in the cellars; and the dirt and rottenness of the place; are not distant but fresh memories. They are all before me, just as they were in the evil hour when I went among them for the first time, with my trembling hand in Mr Quinion's.

1 Which words tell us that the building was in poor condition?
2 How clearly does David remember how he felt?
3 What tells us he felt nervous?

PARAGRAPH 2

Murdstone and Grinby's trade involved lots of activities, but an important part of it was the supply of wines and spirits to ships. I know that a great many empty bottles were one of the consequences of this trade, and that certain men and boys were employed to examine them against the light, reject those that were damaged, and to rinse and wash the others. When the empty bottles ran short, there were labels to be pasted on full ones, or corks to be fitted to them, or seals to be put upon the corks, or finished bottles to be packed. All this work was my work, and I was one of the many boys employed to do it.

4 Say, in your own words, what Murdstone and Grinby's business was.
5 What were David's duties?
6 How would you feel if you were David?

5 Look at these questions. Which have ironic replies?

1 A: Did you have a good holiday?
   B: It was wonderful (it rained and our car was stolen).
2 A: What was the food like?
   B: It was terrible (everything tasted burnt).
3 A: How is your brother?
   B: He has never been better (he has got a broken leg).

PARAGRAPH 3

> There were four of us, including myself. My working place was established in a corner of the warehouse, where Mr Quinion could see me, when he chose to stand up on the bottom rail of his stool in the counting-house, and look at me through a window above the desk. Here, on the first morning of my so auspiciously beginning working life, the oldest of the regular boys was called to show me my business. His name was Mick Walker, and he wore a ragged apron and a paper cap.

7 Whereabouts did David work and where was he supervised?
8 Who taught David what to do?

PARAGRAPH 4

> No words can express the secret pain of my soul as I sank into this companionship; and felt my hopes of growing up to be a learned and distinguished man crushed in my chest. The sense of hopelessness and shame cannot be written. As often as Mick Walker went away in the course of that morning, I mixed my tears with the water in which I was washing the bottles; and sobbed as if my heart was in danger of bursting.

9 What did David think about his ambition of becoming an educated man?
10 What did he do when he was left alone?

DEVELOPING VOCABULARY

6 Dickens tells us that David's hand was *trembling*, and that he *sobbed* when he was left alone. Read the definitions for other verbs of *moving* and *crying*. Then complete the sentences below.

MOVING
shake (v): **shook/shaken**: to move up and down or from side to side with quick short movements
tremble (v): to shake uncontrollably with quick short movements, usually from fear or anger
shiver (v): to shake, especially because of the cold

CRYING
sob (v): to cry, making short bursts of sound as one breathes in, because of sadness or fear
wail (v): to cry out with a long sound as if in grief or pain
weep (v): **wept/wept** formal or literary – to cry tears

1 He ..... in short painful breaths as he held the broken toy in his arms.
2 The people ..... with cold as they waited for the bus to arrive.
3 It was terrifying to hear the mourners as they ..... at the funeral.
4 She could not point the gun because her arm was ..... so violently.
5 The hotel ..... as the bombs went off across the street.
6 The clown sat by the side of the ring and ..... silently, his tears ruining his make-up.

WRITING

7 Work in pairs. Look at Patrick's basic description of his worst job. Rewrite it, giving the idea of how unpleasant the job really was.

❝The worst job I had was in a butcher's shop. I had to put the heads and the claws of chickens into big barrels. The worst thing was when I had to clean the fridge. A horrible boy locked me in. I was alone in a fridge full of dead animals. I hated it.❞

8 Think of the worst job you have had (or invent one). Make notes under these headings.

a) The building, its location and construction.
b) Your feelings about it now.
c) The nature of the organisation/company.
d) Your boss and colleagues.
e) How you learned to do the job.
f) Your feelings on the first day.

Write your account using a good range of narrative tenses and try to experiment with irony.

Grammar reference

1   *Unless, only if, otherwise*

- The conjunction *unless* means 'except if' or 'if ... not' and introduces a condition.
  EXAMPLE: *I won't speak to him again **unless he apologises**.*

- *Only ... if* makes the condition which follows stronger. *Only* is placed before the main verb.
  EXAMPLE: *I will **only speak** to him again **if** he apologises.*

  Alternatively, *only* can be placed in front of the conjunction *if* with no change of meaning.
  EXAMPLE: *I will speak to him again **only if he apologises**.*

  This form is commonly used in short answers.

- *Otherwise* can be used as a conjunction, to express what will happen (the consequence) if someone doesn't do something. It can either follow a comma, or start a new sentence.
  EXAMPLES: *He'd better apologise, **otherwise** I won't speak to him again.*
  *I hope he apologises. **Otherwise** I won't speak to him again.*

2   Narrative past tenses

- The past simple is often used in narratives to describe a sequence of completed actions.
  EXAMPLES: *I quickly **dressed** and **left** the flat.*
  *He **came in**, **sat down** and **turned on** the television.*

- The past progressive is often used in narratives to set the scene,
  EXAMPLE: *It **was raining** hard and the traffic **was creeping** along the High Street.*

  and to describe an action or situation that was in progress when something else happened.
  EXAMPLES: *I **was crawling** around under the table when there was a stampede.*
  *He **was working** at MAP Advertising when he first met Julia Marsh.*

- The past perfect simple is used to make it clear that a completed action happened before another one, or before a certain time, in the past.
  EXAMPLES: *When he finally arrived, she **had left** and **gone** home.*
  *By the time he arrived, she **had left** and **gone** home.*
  *By seven o'clock, she **had given up** waiting and **gone** home.*

  Notice how the second event (*he arrived*) is expressed in the past simple. The conjuctions *when* and *by the time* are often used in this kind of sentence.

- The past perfect progressive is used to describe a continuous action that had started before a particular time or event in the past, and was still in progress.
  EXAMPLES: *When he finally arrived, she **had been waiting** for over two hours.*
  *By seven o'clock, she **had been waiting** for over two hours.*

  The past perfect progressive is formed with *had been* + the *-ing* form.

GRAMMAR AND FUNCTIONS

1 Respond to the sentences using the present perfect and the superlative form.

This cake is wonderful.
In fact/good cake/I ever eat.
In fact, it's the best cake I've ever eaten.

1 This book is interesting.
   In fact/fascinating book/I ever read.
2 What a lovely dress!
   In fact/it be/beautiful dress/I ever see.
3 This perfume smells awful!
   In fact/disgusting perfume/I ever smell.

2 Complete the sentences by putting each verb into an appropriate past tense.

1 It (be) a beautiful spring morning and the birds (sing). Sheila (get) out of bed and (feel) happy to be alive.
2 I (rush) home to give Bob the message, but I (be) too late. He already (left).
3 When Maria eventually (turn up), I (be) very annoyed – I (wait) for nearly an hour.
4 Nothing could have prepared him for what he (see) when he (open) his eyes.
5 Paul (be) exhausted because he (play) tennis all afternoon.

3 Choose the best word or phrase to complete each sentence. There is one more than you need.

because   otherwise   as a result   owing to
only if   unless

1 Joe had a serious climbing accident. . . . . . , he was unable to work for five months.
2 Joe was unable to work for five months . . . . . he had had a serious climbing accident.
3 You'd better do what the doctor says, ... you'll end up in hospital.
4 You'd better do what the doctor says . . . . . you want to end up in hospital.
5 . . . . . his serious climbing accident, Joe was unable to work for five months.

4 Complete each sentence with either *a, the* or no article (–).

1 We're going to buy her . . . . . piano for her birthday; she already plays . . . . . violin.
2 It's . . . . . marvellous escape story. Do you realise that . . . . . man who wrote it was . . . . . prisoner in . . . . . most notorious camp of all during the Second World War?
3 . . . . . women are generally safer drivers than . . . . . men.
4 There was . . . . . interesting programme about . . . . . Lake Titicaca last night.
5 . . . . . money can't buy . . . . . happiness.
6 I heard . . . . . strange noise from outside my window. As . . . . . noise grew louder I went outside to take a look. It was . . . . . funniest-looking bird I had ever seen.
7 Is this . . . . . record you were telling me about yesterday? I'll listen to it at . . . . . earliest opportunity.
8 After their plane crashed in . . . . . Atlantic, ... survivors lived on . . . . . diet of . . . . . fish and . . . . . rainwater.

VOCABULARY

5 Which four natural disasters are described in these situations?

1 The loud bang from the hunter's gun made the snow and rocks fall onto the village below, completely destroying it.
2 They were waiting to be served in the restaurant when the ground started to move and the glasses fell over and broke. Everybody screamed in terror.
3 It hasn't rained for two years. Nothing can grow and all the animals have died of thirst and hunger.
4 People watched anxiously as the river rose each day. On Sunday evening they evacuated their houses.

Sporting legends

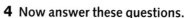

Focus

TOPIC
• Sport

GRAMMAR
• *Wish* + past simple, past perfect, *could*, *would*
• *If only*

SKILLS
• Reading: a newspaper article
• Speaking: role play
• Listening: a monologue
• Writing: sentences

SPEECH PATTERNS
• Expressing desires and regrets: stress

GETTING STARTED

1 Work in pairs. Discuss these questions.

1 Look at these pictures of famous sportsmen and women. What do you think will happen to them when their sporting careers are over?

2 What pressures do you think highly-paid sportspeople are under?

↻ COMPARING CULTURES

2 Think of people in your own country who have continued to be successful or who have had problems since their sporting careers ended.

📷 Documentary

READING

3 Read about Justin Fashanu.

Justin Fashanu has been involved in football all his working life. When he was just nineteen, Fashanu was big news in the national newspapers. Read the article quickly and find out why.

4 Now answer these questions.

1 Were many teams trying to employ Fashanu?
2 How did he feel about his new manager?
3 What experience had he had of different clubs?
4 What do you think it felt like for Fashanu to be the object of so much attention?

Forest's Fashanu

JUSTIN FASHANU, Norwich's England B striker, signed for Nottingham Forest in a £1 million deal last night.

Forest manager Brian Clough completed the deal at 11 p.m. in a hotel near Peterborough, hours before leaving on the club's tour of Spain today.

Fashanu, wanted by a number of clubs, will join Forest in their warm-up matches in Zaragoza.

'I couldn't really have a bigger challenge than the one now facing me,' he said after signing. 'I was aware that other clubs were interested, but I had a choice and my decision was to join Forest.

'I hadn't met Brian Clough before but he impressed me. He's obviously a winner and he makes those around him winners too.

'I'm very satisfied that my future has been settled, but obviously I'm a little sad to be leaving Norwich.

'Norwich is all I have known in football, but certain moves have to be made in life and I just hope that I have made the right one.'

LISTENING

5 📼 **Listen and read. Justin Fashanu talks about Torquay United. Correct the facts in this summary.**

Although it is a small club there are more than 3,000 supporters. The team is full of experienced players. He'd like to buy younger players, but the club isn't very rich. He likes the players a lot and is generally satisfied with the club's performance.

6 📼 **Justin describes his hopes for his new team. Are these statements true or false?**

1 Torquay has lots of enthusiastic supporters.
2 People expect too much too quickly.
3 Supporters tolerate the team's weaknesses.

7 📼 **Justin talks about his regrets.**

1 What are his three big regrets about his career?
2 According to Justin, what is more difficult than becoming successful?
3 What do you think he would do if he could start his career again?

DISCOVERING LANGUAGE

8 Read these sentences from the interview.

A 'I **wish** that people **were** a little bit more tolerant.'
B 'I **wish** I'**d won** a full England cap.'
C 'I **wish** that the support for the team **was** more passionate.'
D 'I **wish** that **I hadn't moved** to Nottingham Forest for a million pounds quite as quickly.'

1 Which sentences express a regret about the past? Which express a desire for change in the present?
2 Complete these rules:
   a) We use *wish* + ... to express a desire for change in the present.
   b) We use *wish* + ... to express a regret about the past.
3 Look at sentence E.
   E 'If **only** I could improve my serve.'
   a) Does this sentence refer to the past or the present?
   b) Is the speaker happy with his/her ability? Do you think he/she has tried to improve it?
   NOTE: We can't say: 'I wish I would improve my serve.'
4 Look at sentence F.
   F 'I wish someone would score a goal.'
   a) Is the speaker talking about the past, present or near future?
   b) Is the speaker confident that this will happen?

SPEECH PATTERNS

9 📼 **Sentences A–F in Exercise 8 all emphasise a desire or a regret. Which words do you think will be stressed? Listen to the cassette to check. Then repeat the sentences, stressing the correct words.**

WRITING

10 Write sentences using *I wish* or *If only* about these situations.

1 It's almost the end of the match and your team is winning. You want the game to end.
2 Your team lost the match because you let an easy goal through.
3 You are watching your favourite sportsperson. You would like to be able to play like him/her.
4 You are watching a match, but the sun where you are sitting is too hot. You'd like to sit in the shade, but you can't move.
5 You stopped having tennis lessons when you were young. You regret this now.
6 The supporters in front of you keep waving an enormous flag so you can't see the match.
7 You can't play in the basketball team because you aren't tall enough. How do you feel about your height?

SPEAKING

11 Work in pairs.
Student A: You are a journalist. Interview your partner for a magazine article about his/her career. Find out:

a) when he/she started to play. Who influenced and encouraged him/her.
b) what his/her ambitions are. How he/she feels about the future.
c) any disappointments or regrets he/she has about his/her career so far.

Student B: Turn to page 128 and use the information to answer your partner's questions.

Winning and losing

Focus

TOPIC
• Sports psychology

GRAMMAR
• Adverbs and adjectives

SKILLS
• Listening: an interview
• Reading: a magazine article
• Speaking: conversations

VOCABULARY DEVELOPMENT
• Suffixes

GETTING STARTED

1 Read the statements and answer the questions.

A Playing fair and being a good sport are more important than winning.

B Winning isn't everything. It's the *only* thing.

C *Winning or losing don't matter; it's playing the game that counts.*

D 'Show me a good loser and I'll show you a loser.'

1 What kind of people would say these things?
2 Which statement is closest to your own attitude?

☸ COMPARING CULTURES

2 Work in pairs. Discuss these questions.

1 In Britain, many people believe that playing fair and being a good sport are more important than actually winning! How important is it to be a winner or a 'good sport' in your country?
2 Do your national teams have the reputation of being winners or losers?

LISTENING

3 Dr Marion Stacey, a sports psychologist, is being interviewed about her work. Before you listen, discuss these questions.

1 What does a sportsperson need in order to succeed at the very highest levels?
2 Why do you think so many top sportspeople use sports psychologists?
3 A top tennis professional keeps losing important matches. What could be causing this problem and how could a psychologist help?

4 ▦ Listen and make notes.

1 What three things must top sportspeople have?
2 What is the difference between individual and team sports?
3 Make notes about the difficulties a tennis player was having and how Dr Stacey helped.

SPEAKING

5 Discuss these questions.

1 How convinced were you by Dr Stacey and her treatment?
2 Is there anything that you would use a sports psychologist for?

DEVELOPING VOCABULARY

6 In the interview with Dr Stacey there are lots of words which use suffixes. Add suffixes to the words in *italics*.

What do you call the period when one is a *child*? *childhood*

1 If someone is behaving like a naughty child, we tell them not to be *child* ...
2 If something is moving down, it moves *down* ...
3 If something is of help, it is *help* ...
4 If something is without hope, it is *hope* ...
5 If it is possible to teach something, it is *teach* ...
6 Make nouns from these words:
   a) fit: *fit* ...
   b) to excite: *excite* ...

Think of other words which have the same suffixes.

READING

7 Before you read, discuss these questions.

1 Are there basic differences in the brains of men and women which make men better at games like chess?
2 Do sporting, musical or intellectual talent depend on inheritance or education and upbringing?

THE CHESS PRINCESS

Several theories have tried to explain why women aren't as good at chess as men. One theory claims that the right hemisphere of the brain, which deals with spatial relationships, is more dominant in men. Another even suggests that women find it difficult to concentrate because they are genetically programmed to hear the cry of a child!

■ ■ ■

Lately, Laszlo Polgar from Hungary has disproved these theories by turning his daughters Zsusza, Zsofia and Judit into chess geniuses. The sisters recently beat a strong Russian team. Ex-psychology teacher Polgar has used the new 'hot-house' training techniques to educate his children. At first he did consider producing musicians, but decided chess was cheaper. He says his techniques can be applied to other mental disciplines – but what counts is to start very early. From the age of four the girls trained in chess and languages. They hardly went to school at all and were educated at home.

■ ■ ■

Of the three, Judit is the most remarkable: at the age of twelve she beat senior male competitors to become an international grand master. This is like a woman athlete winning a gold medal in a men's event. One explanation of her success is that she has an intuitive grasp of the position of a game. She does not have to think logically, but can make moves intuitively in the same way as gifted musicians 'see' music.

■ ■ ■

Hot-housing in sport *has* produced successes like child gymnasts, but it has its victims too. Is it justifiable to use children as guinea pigs, or pawns in your own game? Polgar has nearly achieved his dream of manufacturing a woman world champion, but at what future cost to his children?

8 Read the article and find out whether it confirms or contradicts your ideas.

9 Now answer these questions.

1 What does the author think about the second theory in Paragraph 1?
2 What motivated Polgar to do what he did?
3 Why is Judit's achievement compared with athletics?
4 How does the writer explain Judit's success?
5 How does the writer really feel about Polgar?

REVIEWING LANGUAGE

10 Look at this sentence from the text.

They hardly went to school at all.

1 How often did they go to school?
2 In the groups below, which words in **bold** type are adjectives and which are adverbs?
   a) She works **hard**.
   b) It's **hard** work.
   c) She **hardly** works.
   d) It's a **late** performance.
   e) We arrived **late**.
   f) Has he seen her **lately**?
   g) They are **nearly** ready.
   h) They live quite **near**.
   i) They are **near** neighbours.
3 Which adverb means:
   a) almost?   b) recently?   c) very little?

11 Using the adverbs in Exercise 10, rephrase the words in *italics* in these sentences.

We're *not far from* home *now*, only a few more miles.
We're nearly home now, only a few more miles.

1 I *almost* passed the exam; I failed by two marks.
2 I've been feeling tired *for the past few weeks*.
3 I'm worried about Maria; she eats *so little*.
4 He *can't* hear *very well at all*.
5 Have you read any good books *in the last month*?
6 *I'll finish the exercise soon*, can you wait?

SPEAKING

12 Work in pairs. Take turns to read and respond to the rephrased sentences. Build a short conversation around each situation.

51

Sensational Sumo

Fight of the pure

The clay fighting ring is itself a sacred shrine. On entering it, the *rikishi* first claps to attract the gods' attention and indicate his own purity of heart. Then he shakes his apron to drive away evil spirits, and raises his arms to show he carries no weapons. Next comes his most dramatic gesture, *shiko*. With his left hand on his heart and his right hand extended to the east, the huge fighter raises his right leg as high as possible – to send it crashing down with all his force. Then he performs the same earth-shaking stamp with the other leg. After that, the *rikishi* purifies himself and the ring by throwing salt, wiping himself, and rinsing his mouth with water. Finally, the opponents spend three or four minutes trying to intimidate each other with grimaces and threatening postures.

Seconds out

The fight itself is brief and brutal. The wrestlers may not punch with a clenched fist, pull hair, poke eyes, kick to the stomach, grab the front part of the loincloth, or choke their opponents. Anything else is fair game. The result is a thunderous collision that rarely lasts more than ten seconds. The *rikishi* hurl themselves at each other, and the contest ends when one giant is pushed to the ground or outside the circle, which is 4.6 m (15 ft) in diameter.

Article from *Mountain Men,* Reader's Digest 1990

Focus

TOPICS
- Sumo wrestling
- New games

SKILLS
- Reading: articles
- Writing: procedures

VOCABULARY DEVELOPMENT
- Sequencers
- Words of noise, size and violent movement

Describing procedures

SPEAKING

1 The men in the picture are Sumo wrestlers. What do you know about this sport?

READING

2 Now read these notes. How is Sumo different from most other sports?

- Sumo, Japan's oldest martial art, is over 2,000 years old. In ancient times fights could be to the death!
- It is connected with the ancient Shinto religion.
- Japan has 800 *rikishi* (professional wrestlers).
- The average *rikishi* weighs 135 kg; the heaviest ever weighed 252 kg (equal to four ordinary men).
- A special diet helps put weight on the lower body.
- Sumo wrestlers have to be able to move very fast.

3 Read part of an article (above) about Sumo and make questions for these answers.

1 To drive away evil spirits.
2 To purify the ring and himself.
3 To try and scare his opponent.
4 Usually under ten seconds.
5 When one of them is pushed out of the ring or falls over.

DEVELOPING VOCABULARY

4 Find the words and images the writer uses to describe size, noise and violent movement.

5 Read Paragraph 1 again. How many ways of putting events in order are there?

READING

6 Before you read, look at these new sports. What do you think they can be?

7 Read the article and decide which sport it describes. Make notes under the headings in the chart. The gaps are filled in Exercise 8.

AIM:	EQUIPMENT: ..... SCORING: .....
NUMBER OF PLAYERS:	PROCEDURE: .....

Deciding the rules

As with most other competitive games, ¹..... 'Sticky' is to score the most points. Now, ²..... is by jumping on the trampoline and then throwing yourself against the wall and sticking there. ³..... play 'Sticky' you need some special equipment: a tracksuit covered with velcro – that special kind of material which is used to fasten things, a trampoline and the sticky wall which is covered in velcro too. You also have to wear a helmet and goggles to protect your head and eyes. ⁴..... to the actual game. ⁵..... you stand on the platform and jump onto the trampoline. ⁶..... three bounces before you launch yourself onto the special wall. You're not allowed to change your position after the jump and have to stick in position for at least five seconds. ⁷..... the referee gives each player points. ⁸..... get the most is by landing up high and upside down!

8 Complete the rules in Exercise 7 using these words and expressions.

afterwards   the way you do this
first of all   the object of
you're allowed   the way to
in order to   let's move on

FOCUS ON STYLE

9 Look at the text again.

1 What form of the verb is mostly used: active or passive?
2 Which pronoun is used to give instructions?
3 Is the style formal or informal?

WRITING

10 Work in pairs or groups. Choose one of the other sports and make notes for a set of rules.

11 Using your notes and the articles about 'Sticky' and Sumo wrestling as a guide, write your own set of rules.

Grammar reference

1 Wish

- We use *wish* + past simple to express a regret about a present situation by imagining its opposite.
  EXAMPLES: *I **wish** I **lived** by the sea.* (but I don't)
  *I **wish** I **could play** the piano.* (but I can't)
  *I **wish** I **was rich**.* (but I'm not)
  As in second conditional sentences, *were* is often used instead of *was* in the first and third person singular, especially in formal English.
  EXAMPLE: *I **wish** he **were** with me now.*

- We use *wish* + *would* to express a desire for change in the near future, especially when someone or something is annoying us.
  EXAMPLES: *I **wish** it **would** stop raining.*
  *I **wish** you **would** be quiet.*
  *I **wish** you **wouldn't** wear that stupid hat.*

- Wishes about ourselves cannot be expressed with *would*. We have to use *could* or *I hope*.
  EXAMPLES: *I **wish** I **could** lose weight.* (NOT *I wish I would ...*)
  *I **hope** we get there on time.* (NOT *I wish we would ...*)

- We use *wish* + past perfect to express a regret about something in the past. We are imagining the opposite of what actually happened.
  EXAMPLES: *I **wish** I **had listened** to his advice.* (but I didn't)
  *I **wish** I **hadn't eaten** three pieces of chocolate cake!* (but I did!)

2 If only ... !

- We can use *If only* instead of *I wish* to express stronger feelings of regret or stronger wishes:
  EXAMPLES: ***If only** I lived by the sea!*
  ***If only** I'd listened to his advice!*
  ***If only** he wouldn't wear that stupid hat!*
  ***If only** I could lose weight!*

3 Hardly, lately and nearly

- The adverb *hardly* means 'almost not'.
  EXAMPLES: *It was so dark that we **could hardly** see.*
  *I **hardly** ever **have time** to watch television.*
  *I've **hardly slept** since I heard the news.*
  Notice that *hardly* comes before the main verb, but after auxiliary verbs, modal verbs and the verb *to be*.
  Remember that the adverb from the adjective *hard* is *hard*. It has no connection with *hardly*.
  EXAMPLE: *You shouldn't work so **hard**, you know.*

- *Hardly* is often used with *any* and its compounds.
  EXAMPLES: *I've got **hardly any** money left.* (= almost no money)
  ***Hardly anyone** turned up for the meeting.* (= almost no one)
  *I've had **hardly anything** to eat all day.* (= almost nothing)

- The adverb *lately* means the same as *recently*. However, it is used only in the present perfect tense, and is most often used with questions and negatives.
  EXAMPLES: *Have you seen any good films **lately**?*
  *I haven't been sleeping well **lately**.*
  Notice the position of *lately* at the end of the sentence.
  Remember that the adverb from the adjective *late* is *late*. It has no connection with *lately*.
  EXAMPLE: *She always turns up **late** for the class.*

- The adverb *nearly* means the same as *almost*.
  EXAMPLES: *I've **nearly finished**.*
  *I **nearly forgot** to go to the meeting.*
  *Her dress **was nearly** the same colour as mine.*
  Like *hardly*, *nearly* comes before the main verb, but after auxiliary verbs, modal verbs and the verb *to be*.

- *Nearly* is not used with negative words such as *no, nothing, never*. We cannot say:
  * There's nearly no milk left in the fridge.
  Instead, we say:
  *There's **hardly any** milk left in the fridge.*
  Remember that the adverb from the adjective *near* is *near*.
  EXAMPLE: *She lives quite **near** me.*

Talkback

Versions

1 Work in groups. Use the pictures to invent a story in the past using narrative tenses. Use at least seven of the pictures. If you like, you can invent two more pictures for the story. First decide what kind of story it will be, (e.g. a horror story, a thriller, a romance).

2 Now make new groups. Take turns to tell your story. Remember to use a range of narrative tenses in the past.

A helping hand

Focus

TOPIC
• Guest relations

GRAMMAR
• First and second conditionals

SKILLS
• Reading: a questionnaire
• Speaking: discussing a questionnaire/ organising a party/negotiating/ role play
• Listening: a monologue

Doing the right thing

GETTING STARTED

1 Imagine you are in a busy theme park or fairground. What would you do in the following situations?

1 You are leaving the park with a group of young children when you notice a small girl who is obviously lost and unhappy. Would you:
a) pretend not to see her?
b) ask another adult to help?
c) spend time looking for her parents?

2 Some teenagers are trying to force a small child onto a fast and terrifying ride. Would you:
a) take no notice?
b) try to stop them?
c) call someone official?

3 You see a pickpocket about to take a wallet from a man's back pocket. Would you:
a) tell the man?
b) try to stop the thief?
c) try to find a police officer?

4 You have been queuing for ages for a ride when some disabled people are led to the front of the queue. Would you:
a) say they should queue?
b) think it was OK?
c) insist that you go first?

2 Work in pairs. Compare your answers.

REVIEWING LANGUAGE

3 Look at this sentence.

   A *If you saw a pickpocket, would you try to stop him?*

1 Which conditional is sentence A? Does it describe an event in the past?
2 Look at sentence B. Which conditional is this?

   B *If you see my cousin, will you tell her I want to see her?*

3 Which forms of the verb are used in sentences A and B, in:
a) the *if* clause?   b) the main clause?
4 Which sentence, A or B, describes:
   – something that is likely to happen?
   – an imaginary situation?

4 Expand the prompts to form conditional sentences. The more probable something is, the higher the percentage.

If/she/fail exam(80%)/have to leave university
If she fails the exam, she'll have to leave university.

1 If/we/take no notice (80%)/teenagers/ force/child/on the ride
2 It/be/insensitive/if/we/complain about disabled people going to the front of the queue (10%)
3 You/get hurt/if/try to stop/thief (70%)
4 You/regret it/if/pretend not/see her (30%)

SPEAKING

5 Imagine you are organising a party for a group of about thirty people of different ages. Decide on the type and style of party you want. Individually, number the choices in each category in order of your own preference.

DRESS
quite formal: smart clothes . . . . .
fancy dress: where you wear a costume . . . . .
informal: jeans . . . . .

MUSIC
pop music . . . . .   jazz . . . . .   classical/opera . . . . .

FOOD
sit down meal inside   . . . . .   buffet   . . . . .
outside barbecue . . . . .

ENTERTAINMENT
karaoke singing . . . . .   folk songs   . . . . .
disco/dancing   . . . . .   party games . . . . .

TIME
lunchtime . . . . .   evening (7.00–10.00) . . . . .
night (11.00 +) . . . . .

---

6 Work in groups of three or four. Compare your answers and negotiate a format for the party which will satisfy everybody in your group.

🖻 Documentary

7 Read the following and answer the question.
Universal Studios Florida is a theme park and the biggest movie studio outside California. It has rides and shows based on films made there and attracts thousands of visitors each day. Look at the picture of Tina Sonnier. What do you think her job is?

LISTENING

8 Before you listen, match the duties below with the illustrations.

a) warming babies' bottles
b) giving foreign language information
c) helping visitors plan their day
d) pushing wheelchairs
e) picking up litter
f) assisting people who are sick

Which duties do you think Tina has to do? Can you think of any others?

📼 Now listen to Tina and check if your guesses were correct.

9 📼 Tina talks about an occasion when she helped a family. The mother was suffering from the disease multiple sclerosis (MS). Listen to this section and answer these questions.

1 How old was the woman and her family?
2 Why had her husband contacted Universal Studios in advance?
3 How did the 'back door card' help everybody?
4 Why did guest relations suggest that the family should split their daily visit into two?

10 📼 Listen to Tina talking about the difficulties of her job.

1 What is the most difficult thing about her job?
2 How does she try to make herself feel better about it?

SPEAKING

11 Work in pairs.
Make a list of all the questions and complaints that Tina has to deal with every day.

Student A: Choose one item from your list. You are going to see Tina about it. Choose from one of these attitudes: happy, angry, frightened, sick.

Student B: You are Tina Sonnier. Respond to your partner as helpfully as possible. Of course, you have to be polite all the time.

The best of intentions

Focus

TOPIC
• Emergencies

GRAMMAR
• Third conditional

SKILLS
• Listening: a story
• Reading: newspaper articles
• Speaking: role play

VOCABULARY DEVELOPMENT
• Action words

GETTING STARTED

1 Look at the cartoon and say what you think has happened.

📟 Now listen to the story to see if you were right.

THANKS DOC! PENKNIFE OP SAVES JACK ON JET

Cut throat stops him choking

LUCKY Jack Sykes said a big thank you yesterday to the doctor who saved his life with a penknife op five miles up in a jet.

Quick-thinking Charles Plotkin dashed to the rescue when 88-year-old Jack slumped unconscious – a piece of chicken stuck in his throat. If the doctor hadn't operated, Jack would have died.

Passengers feared Jack was dead. But US Air Force anaesthetist Charles carefully selected a blade from a borrowed Swiss Army penknife. Then he slashed a hole in Jack's neck, pushed the meat loose and got him breathing again. And last night the fully-recovered pensioner admitted: 'Without him I would have been a goner.

But I never got the chance to thank him.'

Jack added: 'My wife has sent him a letter of thanks and I'm writing to his commanding officer praising his quick thinking and skill.' Jack and his wife Averina, 78, were on their way to a diamond wedding party in Texas when drama struck on the flight from Syracuse to San Antonio.

READING

2 Work in two groups. One group reads Article A, and the other Article B. Complete the chart for your article only.

	ARTICLE A	ARTICLE B
Type of emergency	. . . . .	. . . . .
Victim	. . . . .	. . . . .
When/where took place	. . . . .	. . . . .
Action doctor took	. . . . .	. . . . .
Patient's reaction	. . . . .	. . . . .
Effectiveness of action	. . . . .	. . . . .
How doctor felt afterwards	. . . . .	. . . . .
How patient felt	. . . . .	. . . . .

3 Find a partner from the other group and tell each other about the story you have read. Complete the rest of the chart.

Passing GP gives mock crash victim the needle

A doctor rushed to the rescue when he stumbled on what he thought was the scene of a rail disaster. Dr Robert Lambourn burst through a police cordon and dashed into the nearest carriage where he saw a man with a serious leg wound lying face down, apparently semi-conscious.

As he prepared to inject the man with a powerful painkiller, the victim said: 'Do we really have to go that far?'

As his patient fell unconscious, he whispered he was perfectly healthy and taking part in a training exercise. The man, in his early twenties, was taken to hospital for treatment. Of course, the doctor wouldn't have given the injection if he had known it was an exercise.

Dr Lambourn was driving to his surgery when he came across the rail crash near his home village. Two trains had apparently collided head-on. Sixty bodies lay scattered through the wreckage and at the trackside. A police helicopter was overhead but the ambulances had not arrived. Dr Lambourn parked, grabbed his bag and, telling police he was a doctor, went into action.

Mrs Merle Latham, of the regional St John Ambulance brigade, said:'The victim was covered in blood and a great piece of bone was sticking out through his trousers. The poor doctor wasn't to know the bone was just something picked up from a butcher.'

DEVELOPING VOCABULARY

4 Find these six verbs in the reports.

slump   slash   dash   rush   burst   grab

Match each verb with the correct meaning.

1 to take hold of something suddenly
2 to run suddenly and quickly
3 to hurry
4 to cut with a violent stroke
5 to sink down or fall heavily
6 to enter/pass through suddenly and unexpectedly

5 Complete the text, using each verb from Exercise 4 once only.

At three a.m. the police ¹..... into Watson's hotel room. He jumped up from his bed and ²..... towards the door. He ³..... a large knife and ⁴..... viciously at the inspector. A constable hit Watson on the head and he ⁵..... unconscious to the floor. They ⁶..... him to hospital where he quickly recovered.

DISCOVERING LANGUAGE

6 Look at this third conditional sentence from the text and answer the questions.

If the doctor hadn't operated, Jack would have died.

1 How is the third conditional formed?
2 Did the doctor operate?
3 Did Jack die?
4 Does all the action happen in the past?
5 Is the situation above real or unreal?

7 Complete these sentences based on the two articles.

1 If he hadn't driven to the surgery, ...
2 If he hadn't thought the man was hurt, he .....
3 He wouldn't have gone to hospital .....
4 The doctor wouldn't have thought he was hurt if .....
5 If he hadn't eaten chicken salad, ...
6 Without a penknife the doctor .....

SPEAKING

8 Read about Chris and Jo's holiday.

When Chris and Jo went on holiday it was a complete disaster. They woke up late. They ran out of petrol on the motorway. They missed their plane. Their luggage got lost. On holiday Jo got sunburnt. All their money was stolen. When they got home the goldfish had died and the house had been burgled.

Work in pairs and blame each other for what went wrong.

JO: *It's your fault – if you had set the alarm clock, we wouldn't have woken up late.*

Student A: You are Jo. You think everything is Chris's fault because Chris:
• forgot to set the alarm clock.
• didn't tie labels on the luggage securely.
• didn't pack the sun cream.
• left a small window in your house open.

Student B: You are Chris. You think everything is Jo's fault because Jo:
• forgot to fill the car with petrol.
• insisted that cash would be better than travellers' cheques.
• forgot to ask a neighbour to feed the goldfish every day.

Expressing a point of view

Focus

TOPIC
• Unlawful actions

FUNCTIONS
• Stating purpose
• Giving opinions
• Emphasising
• Adding information

SKILLS
• Reading: a letter to a newspaper
• Speaking: a discussion
• Writing: a letter to a newspaper

VOCABULARY DEVELOPMENT
• Adjectives formed from adverb + past participle

1 Quickly read the article below. Are these statements true or false?

1 Ian was in his own home.
2 The men struggled all the way through the house.
3 Ian refused to help.
4 The criminal escaped.
5 No action can be taken against Ian.
6 People support him.

BABY-SITTER SITS BACK

Ian Marshall was baby-sitting for a friend when the back door burst open and two men rushed in. A burglar was trying to escape from a policeman who wanted to arrest him.

The two men fought through the house and went out through the front door. Ian rang the police for help, then went outside to see what was happening.

The police officer asked Ian to lend a hand, but he refused and closed the door. The burglar got away.

Ian could be prosecuted under a law which says that a fit and well person who refuses to help the police is guilty of an offence. He could be fined or sent to jail. People in his home town call him a coward.

SPEAKING

2 In pairs or groups, discuss what you think about the case. Consider these points.

1 Does Ian deserve to be called a coward?
2 What would you have done?
3 Generally speaking, what would happen in a similar case in your country?

READING

3 Look at the letter below about the Ian Marshall story, which was printed in a British newspaper.

1 What does the writer think about Ian Marshall's critics?
2 How does she justify what Ian did?
3 What do you think of the writer's attitudes to the risks and rewards of police work?
4 How far do you agree with the ideas of the letter?

Dear Sir,

1- I am writing to speak up in support of Ian Marshall, the member of the public who has been severely criticised for not assisting a policeman trying to arrest a burglar. In my opinion this is unfair.

2- According to the armchair Rambos who criticise him, Ian Marshall should have risked his life restraining a desperate and violent man. This is fine in theory, but how in practice can ordinary peace-loving members of the public be expected to act? On the one hand, it may be

DEVELOPING VOCABULARY

4 Look at these sentences.

*Police officers have **good insurance**.* (adjective + noun)
*They are **well-insured**.* (adverb + participle adjective)

Now rephrase these sentences.

1 Police officers have good training. They are ...
2 The doctor had good intentions. He was ...
3 People have a high regard for Dickens. He is ...
4 Nurses' pay is poor. They are ...
5 The film's production was bad. It was ...

FOCUS ON FUNCTIONS

5 Look at the letter again and answer these questions.

1 What is the purpose of each of the paragraphs?
2 How does Julie O'Connor do the following?
   PARAGRAPH 1
   a) state the purpose of her letter   b) say what her position is
   PARAGRAPH 2
   c) report other people's opinions
   d) compare the 'ideal' world with the 'real' world
   e) balance opposing points of view in the same sentence
   PARAGRAPH 3
   f) give her opinion   g) emphasise something
   h) make an extra point
   PARAGRAPH 4
   i) state a conclusion   j) give her opinion

Have-a-go hero stabbed

WHEN science teacher Robert Jacobs looked out of his window, he saw a young man slashing car tyres.

Grabbing a hammer, he chased the vandal to a block of flats. Stephen Woodward – the young man – was clearly afraid of Jacobs and stabbed him through the heart. He was arrested for murder, but at the trial the jury decided he wasn't guilty on the grounds of self-defence. Woodward is now a free man. Afterwards, the nineteen year old said he wasn't sorry for what he had done. He claimed that he understood how Jacob's family felt because his mother had died. He said that he slashed car tyres for fun and blamed alcohol and being brought up in care for his behaviour.

6 Read about another situation (above) and decide what similarities and differences there are with the Ian Marshall case.

7 Work in pairs or small groups and discuss these questions.

1 What you would have done if you had been Mr Jacobs?
2 Was Jacobs wrong to chase Woodward with a hammer?
3 What you think of the verdict?

WRITING

8 Write a letter to a newspaper about the Stephen Woodward case. Use the letter about the Ian Marshall case as a guide. Organise your letter like this.

PARAGRAPH 1
State the purpose of the letter.
Say generally what you think about the case.

PARAGRAPH 2
Say what you think about the jury's verdict.
Balance the arguments for and against convicting Woodward of murder.

PARAGRAPH 3
Expand on Paragraph 2.

PARAGRAPH 4
Give your conclusion.
State how you would have behaved.

reasonable to expect the public to assist the police, but on the other, the police must accept that such help is purely voluntary.

In my view, police officers accept the hazards of their profession when they join the force and are paid accordingly. Not only are they physically fit, but they are also well-trained in self-defence. What's more, they are well-insured and receive generous payments if they are injured. After all, if Ian had got hurt (or worse) by taking a foolish risk, he wouldn't have received any compensation.

Even though his behaviour wasn't particularly courageous, on balance I agree with what he did, or rather did *not* do. Under similar circumstances I am certain that I wouldn't have had the stomach for a fight either. As far as I'm concerned he was right to put the children and his own safety first. Despite what people may say I am certain that the vast majority would have behaved in a similar way in the same situation.

(Ms) Julie O'Connor

61

Grammar reference

1 First conditional sentences

- We use the first conditional to talk about the consequences of a possible future event which we think is likely to happen.
  EXAMPLE: *If John phones tonight, I'll pretend I'm not at home.* (The speaker thinks it is likely that John will phone.)
- We often use the first conditional to express promises or threats.
  EXAMPLES: *If you're a good boy, I'll buy you an ice cream.*
  If you do that again, I'll phone the police.
- See Grammar reference 5.1 for the use of *unless*, *only if* and *otherwise* with first conditional sentences.

FORM

- The standard form of the first conditional is
  If + present tense clause + *will* + infinitive without *to*:
  If I see him, *I'll give him the letter.*
- Either the *if* clause or the consequence clause can come first. When the *if* clause comes second, there is usually no comma between the clauses.
  EXAMPLE: *I'll give him the letter **if I see him**.*
- See also Grammar reference 12.3 for the use of the future progressive in first conditional sentences.

2 Second conditional sentences

- We use the second conditional to talk about the consequences of an event that is possible but unlikely to happen,
  EXAMPLE: *If I won a million pounds, I'd buy a yacht and sail round the world.*
  or the consequences of an unreal or imaginary situation.
  EXAMPLE: *If I ruled the world, I would end all wars.*
- We also use the second conditional when we want to be less direct in what we say.
  EXAMPLE: *If I washed your car for you, would you let me borrow it?*
- *Were* is often used instead of *was* in the first and third person singular, especially in formal English, and to give advice.
  EXAMPLE: *If I **were** you, I'd see a doctor.*

FORM

- The standard form of the second conditional is
  If + past simple clause + *would* + infinitive without *to*:
  If he apologised, *I **would forgive** him.*
  Notice that, even though the simple past is used, we are not referring to past time.

3 Third conditional sentences

- We use the third conditional to talk about events or situations which are completely in the past and cannot be changed. We are imagining the opposite of what actually happened.
  EXAMPLE: *If he had been more careful, he wouldn't have broken the vase.* (But he wasn't careful, so he broke the vase. Nothing can change this.)
- We often use the third conditional when we want to express regrets and talk about lost opportunities.
  EXAMPLES: *If we'd set off earlier, we wouldn't have missed the train.*
  I would have been more understanding if I'd known she was feeling homesick.
  Notice how the *if* clause is similar to the use of *I wish* and *If only* to express regrets (see Grammar reference 6.1, 6.2).

FORM

- The standard form of the third conditional is
  If + past perfect clause + *would have* + past participle: ***If I'd known*** *he was in town, I **would have invited** him to the party.*
  Be careful: You CANNOT use *would have* in the *if* clause.
- Notice these typical third conditional question forms:
  What would have happened if someone had seen you?
  What would you have done if you'd been in his position?
  Would you have phoned the police (if you'd been in his position)?

4 *May*, *might* and *could* in conditional sentences

- When we are less certain about the consequences, we can use *may* or *might* instead of *will*, and *might* instead of *would* in conditional sentences.
  EXAMPLES: *If it stops raining, I **may/might go** for a walk.*
  *If I won a million pounds, I **might give up** work.*
  *If we'd set off earlier, we **might** not **have missed** the train.*
- We can also use *could* instead of *will* and *would* in first and second conditional sentences.
  EXAMPLE: *If it stops raining, we **could go** for a walk.* (making a suggestion)
  *If I won a million pounds, I **could give** up work.* (but I don't know if I would)

Progress check Units 6–7

1 Imagine the opposite of these situations and write a sentence for each one, beginning with the words given.

1 Your girlfriend/boyfriend lives a long way away.
   If only …
2 Your brother/sister keeps borrowing your clothes without asking you.
   I wish …
3 Unfortunately you can't speak German.
   I wish …
4 You were rude to your teacher yesterday and now you regret it.
   If only …
5 You got up late and think you might miss the train.
   I wish …
6 You are watching a film. Some people behind you keep talking. You want them to stop.
   I wish …

2 Write sentences with *if* about these past situations. Begin with the words you are given.

1 We didn't go swimming because the sea was too cold.
   We …
2 I didn't realise you were waiting. That's why I didn't hurry.
   If …
3 He looked honest so she lent him the money.
   If …
4 Why do you think I agreed to come? Because you told me Pete would be here!
   I …
5 I didn't know it was your cake. That's why I ate it.
   If …
6 Why weren't you more careful? You've broken it!
   If …

3 Make complete sentences by matching the following parts.

1 If you promise to be careful,	a) I'll miss the plane.
2 If I were you,	b) I'll show you how it works.
3 As soon as I get there,	c) what would you do?
4 Unless I leave straight away,	d) I'll phone you.
5 If you were in my position,	e) I wouldn't trust them.

4 Fill each gap in this text with one suitable word.

Have you [1]..... wondered how you [2]..... react [3]..... someone near you needed first aid? My sister [4]..... choked in a restaurant recently and I didn't know what to do. Fortunately someone else did. If the man at the next table [5]..... not acted quickly, my sister [6]..... have died. Preparing ourselves for sudden emergencies like this is something we [7]..... ever think about – until disaster strikes.

VOCABULARY

5 Add a suitable suffix to each word in brackets to complete the sentences.

1 They walked for hours through the (dark) before finally seeing the welcome lights of a distant village.
2 Too much coffee can be (harm).
3 They didn't mean any harm – it was just a (child) game.
4 Silas was alone and (friend), with only his gold for company.
5 Philippa tore open the envelope with great (excite).
6 Don't worry about the tap water. It's perfectly (drink).
7 There's nothing we can do. The situation is (hope).
8 Her (kind) was completely unexpected.

8 *Money*

Focus

TOPIC
• Banks and money

GRAMMAR
• Passive tenses

SKILLS
• Speaking: a discussion
• Listening: a monologue

VOCABULARY DEVELOPMENT
• Words related to money

Banking on you

GETTING STARTED

1 Match the parts of these sentences to form sayings connected with money.

1 A fool and his money
2 Money is the
3 I wouldn't do it
4 Money doesn't
5 If you look after the pennies,

a) grow on trees.
b) for love nor money.
c) the pounds will look after themselves.
d) are soon parted.
e) root of all evil.

2 Which of the expressions from Exercise 1 would you use to comment on these situations?

1 You're watching a TV programme about a man who fights crocodiles for fun.
2 You hear that someone you think is stupid has paid £200 for some jeans.
3 You're reading a newspaper article about two brothers who killed each other over £50.
4 A child you know is saving up for a bicycle, but complains that it is a slow process.
5 Paul wants his parents to buy him a very expensive pair of trainers. They want him to realise that you have to work hard to earn money.

DEVELOPING VOCABULARY

3 Look at the list of words to do with money. Do you know what they mean? Check in a dictionary, if necessary.

expenses allowance wage
grant subsidy the dole
fine pocket money bribe
salary pension fee tip

4 Match these phrases with a word from Exercise 3 to show who receives what.

1 a child from its parents
2 a lawyer from a client
3 a waiter from a satisfied customer
4 a weekly-paid manual worker
5 a monthly-paid teacher
6 a rich playboy from his parents
7 someone who parks their car where they shouldn't
8 a businessman, to pay for hotels and meals
9 a corrupt politician for a favour

The following people who receive money from the government:

10 a student
11 an unemployed person
12 a farmer who has some of his costs paid
13 a retired person

↻ COMPARING CULTURES

5 Read and discuss the following.

In Britain, many people have debts. They may have a mortgage to buy a house or an overdraft at the bank. They often buy things like cars and washing machines on hire purchase or with credit cards. Even though people know they should save, very few do. What is it like in your culture?

🖹 Documentary

LISTENING

6 The Bank of England, Britain's central bank, is also responsible for the design and production of bank notes. Before you listen, imagine that you

are responsible for producing your country's bank notes and discuss these questions.

1 How could you make it difficult for counterfeiters (criminals who copy bank notes) to forge (make illegal copies of) the notes?
2 How has modern technology made the job of the forger easier in recent years?

📠 Now listen to Chris Bailey, who works at the Bank of England, talking about producing bank notes. How closely do your ideas match his?

7 Now answer these questions.

1 How many different ways of paying for something can you think of?
2 In your country, what changes have taken place in:
   a) the way people pay for things?
   b) the way people are paid?

8 📠 Listen and see how closely Britain compares with your own country. How has the changing use of bank notes affected their production by the Bank of England?

DISCOVERING LANGUAGE

9 Look at these passive sentences.

   A *The Royal Mint produces coins, however, bank notes are issued by the Bank of England.*
   B *He was arrested at the airport.*
   C *Most purchases are made by credit card, not cash.*

1 Which of sentences A–C uses the passive because:
   a) the agent (the person performing the action) is unknown, unimportant or too obvious to mention?
   b) the writer wants to focus on a new subject?
   c) the writer wants to emphasise the agent?

2 Look at four more passive sentences and identify which tenses are used. Where possible change them into active sentences.
   D *The colours **are being modified** by experts.*
   E *Anything that is made **can be copied**.*
   F *The design **is going to be changed** by the bank.*
   G *He **should be given** a long sentence by the judge.*

3 Now work out how the passive is formed:
   a) with the present progressive.
   b) with *going* to.
   c) with modals like *can* and *should.*

4 What do *all* the forms of the passive have in common?

10 Change these sentences from active to passive, or passive to active.

1 Scientists will develop a special ink next year.
2 A spy has infiltrated the gang.
3 The police are watching a well-known forger.
4 The design of the bank notes should be changed.
5 We are going to contact the FBI.
6 We can beat the forgers.
7 These notes were forged by a very clever criminal.
8 The banks are improving the notes' design all the time.

SPEAKING

11 Work in groups. Think of all the things that a bank would have to do to win the title of the perfect bank!

When friends fall out

Focus

TOPIC
- Winning money

GRAMMAR
- Future: *will, going to*
- Future in the past: *was/were going to*

FUNCTIONS
- Congratulating
- Commiserating

SKILLS
- Listening: conversations
- Reading: an article
- Speaking: role play

VOCABULARY DEVELOPMENT
- Phrasal verbs

SPEECH PATTERNS
- Congratulating and commiserating: stress and intonation

GETTING STARTED

1 In Britain, lots of people do the football pools in the hope of getting rich quickly. What do people do in your country?

LISTENING

2 📼 Listen to four people talking and complete the chart.

	A	B	C	D
Situation	.....	.....	.....	.....
Character	.....	.....	.....	.....

3 📼 How are the listening passages connected with each other? There are two separate stories. Listen to Passage D again and create the other half of the conversation.

REVIEWING LANGUAGE

4 Look at these comments.

A *I can't believe it! All that money! I'll buy a new car and I'll give some to my brother.*

B *Peter told me you'd won a fortune. What are you going to do with it? So you're going to buy a new car?*

1 In which situation has the person just heard about the money?

2 Which comment expresses:
   a) a decision made at the moment of speaking?
   b) an intention/something that has already been decided?

I'll give some to my brother.

DISCOVERING LANGUAGE

5 Look at Peter's statement.

I was going to tell you, Mr Biggs, but I didn't want to worry you.

1 Did Peter tell Mr Biggs? Did he intend to?

2 Is Peter talking about:
   a) now?   b) the future?
   c) the past?

3 What is the *function* of what Peter says; is it:
   a) an invitation?   c) a warning?
   b) an excuse?   d) an apology?

6 Complete these sentences by putting the verbs in brackets into the correct tense.

1 When they retire, they ..... (move) to France.

2 Why didn't you say that Peter rang? Sorry, I ..... (tell) you, but then I forgot.

3 Can I telephone for a taxi? Don't bother, I ..... (give) you a lift.

4 We ..... (visit) many more places, but in the end there just wasn't enough time.

5 What ..... (you buy) mother for her birthday? I'm not sure, perhaps I ..... (get) her a new handbag.

FOCUS ON FUNCTIONS

7 Look at the sentences below. Which sentences express:

a) sympathy?   b) congratulations?

You lucky thing!   What bad luck.
I'm so pleased for you.   What a pity!
Congratulations!   Oh dear.
That's brilliant!   Well done!
I'm so sorry.

SPEECH PATTERNS

8 📼 Listen to the way the expressions are said.

1 Underline the stressed parts of the sentences.

2 What happens to the voices at the end of each one?

Listen again and repeat the sentences.

9 Now practise expressing sympathy and congratulations. Work in pairs.

Student B: Turn to page 128. Respond to your partner's sentences.

Student A: Read these sentences to your partner, who has to respond spontaneously to them. Decide how you feel when you give the news.

1 My cat was knocked over by a car.
2 I've just won the lottery!
3 Somebody stole my Walkman.
4 Martha has invited me to go to Paris for a month.
5 I'm really sorry, but I lost the book you lent me.
6 I've got a place at medical school.

Respond to your partner's sentences.

READING

10 Quickly read the first paragraph of the newspaper article and answer these questions.

1 Which of the proverbs from page 64, Exercise 1 best describes the situation?
2 What is the reason for the argument?

Bingo Battles

TWO WOMEN who used to be the best of friends have fallen out over a big win at bingo.

Tamara Foxton and 40-year-old Helena Wallace used to play on Friday evenings and they had an agreement to divide any prize money they won between them. Three weeks ago, 56-year-old grandmother Tamara won the national first prize of £63,000. Office worker Helena said, 'We wept with joy when the prize was announced. When I went to her house the following day to talk about splitting the money she said that she had talked about it with her husband Billy and they had decided to keep it. She said the agreement had only ever been an informal one. She offered me three thousand, but I turned it down.'

Tamara's side of the story is rather different:

'I was going to offer her five thousand, but when she turned on me I didn't feel like giving her anything. A month ago, Billy, Helena and I all went to bingo and she won three hundred pounds. She wouldn't split the money three ways and include Billy, even though he had lent her ten pounds to play that evening. I told her I wasn't going to split my winnings any more. Of course, now she says she can't remember the conversation. Billy is retiring soon and now we are looking forward to travelling a bit.

Helena says:

'I always used to look up to Tamara – she always seemed honest. She has really let me down – it's so unfair. She has gone back on an agreement we had. As far as I am concerned it's half or nothing.'

Now read the whole article and make notes about:

a) Helena's reasons why the money should be split.
b) Tamara's excuses.

11 Work in pairs. Discuss these questions.

1 Which of the women do you believe?
2 What would you do if you were Helena?
3 What would happen if the case went to court?

DEVELOPING VOCABULARY

12 Find the phrasal verbs in the text which mean:

1 to have an argument.
2 to reject/refuse.
3 to attack.
4 to wait with pleasure for something to happen.
5 to respect and admire.
6 to disappoint.

Complete these sentences, using each of the phrasal verbs.

1 The dog ..... the postman and bit him.
2 I can't wait to go on holiday, I'm really ..... it.
3 It was an interesting job, but she ..... it ..... because it wasn't well-enough paid.
4 She had promised to take me home, but at the last minute she rang up to say she couldn't do it. She ..... me ..... badly.
5 They ..... over something stupid and haven't spoken to each other since.
6 I really ..... my grandmother; she is kind, honest and always knows what is right.

SPEAKING

13 Work in pairs.

Student A: You are Tamara. You are angry that Helena has told her story to the newspapers. It makes you look dishonest. You remember telling her the agreement to split the money was over. You are prepared to pay her something because the case has upset you and your husband Billy. You *don't* want to be friends with her again.

Student B: You are Helena. Turn to page 128 and study the notes. Argue your case and try to resolve the situation.

A modern version of a classic story

FOCUS ON LITERATURE

1 Read the summary of *Silas Marner*, a novel written by George Eliot in 1861.

1 What is the relationship between:
   a) Godfrey and Dunstan Cass?
   b) Molly and Eppie?
   c) Marner and Eppie?
   d) Nancy Lammeter and Godfrey?
2 How does Marner change at different points in the story?

Silas Marner has to leave his small religious community because he is wrongly accused of theft. He moves to a village where he works as a weaver and leads a lonely life. His only consolation is the gold he saves. In the evening, he takes it from his hiding place and counts it.

In the same village there are two brothers, Godfrey and Dunstan Cass, the sons of a local gentleman. Godfrey is in love with a young woman of the same social background called Nancy Lammeter. However, he is already married to Molly, a woman of low social class. He is ashamed of her. His younger brother Dunstan, blackmails Godfrey to keep his secret.

One night, Dunstan Cass goes to Silas Marner's cottage and steals his gold. Dunstan mysteriously disappears and Marner almost becomes mad when he discovers the loss of his gold.

Later, Godfrey's wife Molly goes with their child to the village to confront Godfrey. The weather is terrible and she collapses and dies in the snow. Her child Eppie wanders into Marner's cottage and falls asleep by the fire. Marner adopts her and brings her up as his own child. The happiness he lost when his gold was taken returns. Years later, Dunstan's skeleton and the gold are found in a pond by Silas's house, where Dunstan drowned on the night of the robbery.

Godfrey, who is now married to Nancy, confesses that he is Eppie's father and tries to claim her. Eppie refuses to leave Silas, whom she regards as her true father, and marries a simple workman.

Focus

TOPIC
- *Silas Marner*

SKILLS
- Reading: literary extracts
- Writing: a summary/dialogue

STYLE
- Finding modern images

VOCABULARY DEVELOPMENT
- Verbs of *looking* and *holding*/ words related to light

SCENE A

Gradually the guineas, the coins, grew to a heap, and Marner took less and less for his own needs, trying to solve the problem of keeping himself strong enough to work sixteen hours while spending as little as possible. Marner wanted the heaps of ten to grow into a square, and then into a larger square; and every added guinea, while this was in itself a satisfaction, bred a new desire. He handled them, he counted them, till their form and colour were like the satisfaction of a thirst to him; but it was at night, after work, that he took them out to enjoy their companionship.

→⋆→⋆→⋆→

1 Why did Marner spend so little on himself? What was his ambition?
2 How was his love of money like an addiction?
3 What tells us he regarded the coins as his friends?

---

2 Read the three scenes and decide which part of the story is described in each. Then answer the questions after each scene.

DEVELOPING VOCABULARY

3 Look at these words from the text.

glimmer   cling   glance   gaze   glow
grasp

Which words describe:

a) ways of looking?   b) ways of holding?
c) different kinds of light?

WRITING

4 Imagine that you are writing a modern-day version of Silas Marner.

1 Where would you set it?
2 What would Marner's job be?
3 What changes would you make to the plot?
4 Would you add any extra characters?
5 Think of both a happy and an unhappy ending.

SCENE B

Turning towards the hearth, where the two logs had fallen apart, and sent out only a red uncertain glimmer, he seated himself on his fireside chair, and was bending to push his logs together, when it seemed to him as if there were gold on the floor in front of the hearth. Gold! – his own gold – brought back to him as mysteriously as it had been taken away! He felt his heart begin to beat violently, and for a few moments he was unable to stretch out his hand and grasp the restored treasure. The heap of gold seemed to glow and get larger beneath his agitated gaze. He leaned forward at last, and stretched out his hand; but instead of hard coin with the familiar resisting outline, his fingers touched soft warm curls. In utter amazement, Silas fell on his knees and bent his head low to examine the marvel: it was a sleeping child – a round, fair thing with soft yellow rings all over its head.

→>←→>←→>←

4 What was Marner's first reaction to what he saw in front of the fire?
5 How was the child's hair different from the lost gold?
6 What tells us he was surprised by his discovery?

SCENE C

Nancy looked at Godfrey with a pained questioning glance. But his eyes were fixed on the floor. She thought there was a word which might perhaps come better from her lips than from his.

'What you say is natural, my dear child – it's natural you should cling to those who've brought you up,' she said, mildly; 'but there's a duty you owe to your legal father. When your father opens his home to you, I think it's right you shouldn't turn your back on it.'

'I can't feel as I've got any father but one,' said Eppie, impetuously, while the tears gathered. 'I've always thought of a little home where he'd sit in the corner and I would look after him. I can't think of any other home. I wasn't brought up to be a lady, and I can't turn my mind to it. I like the working-folks, and their food, and their ways. And,' she ended passionately, while the tears fell, 'I am promised to marry a working-man, who will live with father, and help me to take care of him.'

→>←→>←→>←

7 Why did Nancy speak instead of Godfrey?
8 How did she try to convince Eppie that she should leave Marner?
9 How many reasons did Eppie give in her refusal?

---

5 In groups, write a summary of your modern version. Use the present tense and explain who each character is as you introduce him or her.

FOCUS ON STYLE

6 What vocabulary and images set the original story in the past, e.g. the logs in the hearth? What similar vocabulary and images would you use to set your version in the present?

SPEAKING

7 Now imagine that you are making a film of your modern version.

1 Which actors and actresses would you choose to play these different parts?
2 Which film director would you choose?

WRITING

8 You are now going to write the modern-day version of the meeting in Scene C.

Before you begin, make notes of the advantages and disadvantages the modern-day Eppie would have to take into consideration before either accepting or refusing her real father's offer.

Now write the conversation in dialogue form. Start like this.

NANCY: *I understand how you feel, but think about the man who is your blood relation.*

Grammar reference

1 The passive

We often use the passive:

- when the agent (the person or thing performing the action) is unknown, uninteresting, unimportant or obvious.
  EXAMPLES: *My handbag **has been stolen**.*
  *Yoghurt **is made** from milk.*
  *Five people **have been questioned** about the incident.*
- to avoid beginning a sentence with a complex subject.
  EXAMPLE: *Much of the money **was collected** by enthusiastic staff and pupils at Charlbury Girls' Grammar School.*
- to focus on a new subject.
  EXAMPLE: *The Royal Mint produces coins. Bank notes, however, **are issued** by the Bank of England.*
- in formal English, especially news reports and written descriptions of scientific and other processes, when an impersonal or indirect style is more appropriate.
  EXAMPLES: *Finally, each item **is stamped** with the sell-by date.*
  *A man **has been arrested** for the break-in at Windsor Castle.* (Compare the informal *They've arrested a man for the break-in at Windsor Castle.*)
- to emphasise the agent.
  EXAMPLE: *The new school **will be opened** by the President.*
- We use *by* when we want to include the agent in a passive sentence.
  EXAMPLE: *The lead role **was sung by** Placido Domingo.*

FORM

- The passive is formed with the verb *to be* + the past participle of a transitive verb. Notice how the object of an active sentence becomes the subject of a passive sentence:

ACTIVE: *A boy on a bike*   *delivered*   **the message**.
     subject   +   verb   +   object

PASSIVE:

The message *was*   *delivered*   *by*   *a boy on a bike.*
subject   +   *to be* +   past   + *by* + agent
                  participle

- Remember, however, that the passive is not usually just another form of an active sentence. In fact, some passive sentences have no obvious active form.
  EXAMPLE: *When **was** the telephone **invented**?*

2 Passive infinitives

- Passive infinitive forms (with or without *to*) can be used after *will*, *going to*, modal verbs and other verbs which normally take the infinitive.
  EXAMPLES: *All candidates **will be notified** by post.*
  *The new leisure centre **is going to be opened** by Prince Charles.*
  *Tickets **should be booked** in advance.*
  *I would love **to be invited** to his party!*

3 The passive of progressive tenses

- We can use passive forms of the present progressive and past progressive tenses. We form them with *is/are* + *-ing* form or *was/were* + *-ing* form.
  EXAMPLES: *My car **is being serviced** at the moment.*
  *When we arrived, the hotel **was** still **being built**.*

4 *Will* and *going to*

Will + infinitive is used to express:

- decisions made at the moment of speaking.
  EXAMPLE: *You look tired. I'**ll make** the dinner tonight.*
- predictions and guesses about the future, often with words like *think, expect, know, suppose, be afraid, be sure*.
  EXAMPLES: *I **think** she'**ll get** the job.*
  *Don't worry. I'**m sure** he'**ll turn up**.*
- promises.
  EXAMPLE: *I'**ll phone** you as soon as I arrive.*
- offers of help.
  EXAMPLE: *I'**ll give** you a lift home if you like.*

Going to + infinitive is used to talk about:

- plans and intentions for the future, i.e. things somebody has already decided to do.
  EXAMPLE: *From now on I'**m going to get up** at seven o'clock every day.*
- predictions based on evidence in the present.
  EXAMPLE: *Look at those clouds. It'**s going to rain**.*

5 *Was going to*

- *Was/were going to* + infinitive is used to talk about things we intended to do in the past, but didn't do.
  EXAMPLES: *I **was going to phone** you, but I forgot.*
  *I **was going to tell** him myself, but I never had time.*
  This is a common way of making an excuse and introducing an explanation of why we didn't do something. The explanation itself usually begins with *but*, as in the examples above.
- *Was/were (just) going to ... when ...* is used to talk about an intended action in the past that was prevented by an interruption.
  EXAMPLE: *We **were** just **going to** start eating **when** the phone rang.*

Talkback

Who's to blame?

1 Look at the picture and describe what you think has happened.

2 Read the text and complete the diagram below to show what happened.

Last week Kim Anderson and Bobby Walsh were out riding in a narrow, winding country lane near their village. The hedges by the road are tall and thick and so it is difficult to see very far ahead. A car came round the bend just as farmer Jo Smith was driving a tractor out of a field. The car driver, Chris Black, hooted and swerved to get past the tractor. The noise frightened the horses and Bobby Walsh fell off and hit his/her head. Luckily he/she was wearing a riding hat. When Chris Black saw Bobby lying in the road, he/she braked hard, skidded on some mud on the road and crashed into a tree. Chris wasn't hurt although the car was very badly damaged.

3 Role play. Everyone involved is meeting to decide who was responsible for the accident.

Work in groups of four. Choose one of the four roles on the right and study the information on the role card. Discuss the accident with the others. Criticise the others, but be ready to accept some of the blame (responsibility) yourself.

ROLE PLAY

CHRIS BLACK

You admit that you weren't going slowly. You had an important meeting in the next town. You were telephoning your client to explain why you were late, but you were in perfect control of the car. You insist that you didn't see the horses and riders when you hooted at the tractor driver. You think it was Jo Smith's fault. He/she came out of the field without looking and was busy lighting a cigarette! Also there was a lot of mud on the road. It was Jo's responsibility to clear it up.

ROLE PLAY

JO SMITH

You think it was the others' fault. The riders were going side by side down a narrow lane. They were not paying attention. The driver was going too fast. Of course there was mud on the road. This is the countryside, not the city. You were going to clear it up when you had finished your day's work.

ROLE PLAY

BOBBY WALSH

You think it was the driver's fault. The loud hooting frightened your horse and you were thrown off. You aren't a very experienced rider. You also think it is the farmer's responsibility to cut the hedges so people can see more easily. People have often asked the farmer to cut back the hedges; he/she agrees but does nothing.

ROLE PLAY

KIM ANDERSON

You feel partly responsible because you let Bobby ride a young and lively horse even though he/she is an inexperienced rider. You think you saw the driver with a car phone in his/her hand as he/she was going round the corner. All the same, you are grateful to the driver because he/she avoided your friend.

In the news

And now the good news

Focus

TOPIC
- Bias in the news

GRAMMAR
- Subject/object questions

FUNCTIONS
- Expressing opinions
- Clarifying information
- Giving examples

SKILLS
- Writing: sentences
- Listening: an interview
- Speaking: role play

STYLE
- Modifying nouns

News wars

Forty-six-year-old newsreader Martyn Lewis is at the centre of a storm over the way the TV news is selected.

According to Martyn there isn't a fair balance between good and bad news. Editors who ignore positive stories annoy Martyn, who claims most broadcasts emphasise the negative. On the other hand, Martyn's opinions annoy colleagues who think that their job is to give viewers the facts, not to make them feel better. Older viewers like angel-faced Martyn for his sunny smile and positive outlook. A few years ago pet-lover Martyn wrote two best-selling books about dogs and cats in the news. He also helps to raise money for good causes.

GETTING STARTED

1 Imagine that you are the editors for the main national news programme of the day. Below are six stories which you could broadcast. Decide which four you would choose and which order to put them in.

a) A widowed housewife who recorded a song for her grandchildren has sold a million records.

b) Two foreign tourists and their guide have been killed in an air crash in your country.

c) A factory has closed and 200 people have lost their jobs.

d) An earthquake in a far-off country has killed 800 people. Nobody from your country has been hurt.

e) A family pet has helped a small child wake up after being in a coma for three months.

f) The goalkeeper of your national football team has been accused of accepting bribes.

READING

2 Read the text and find out who Martyn Lewis is and why he is in the news.

3 Work in pairs. Discuss these questions in relation to a recent news broadcast.

1 How many items can you remember?
2 How many were good news?
3 How many were bad news?

⟳ COMPARING CULTURES

4 Work in pairs. Discuss these questions.

What is the balance between good and bad news on TV in your country? Would many people agree with Martyn?

REVIEWING LANGUAGE

5 Match the questions with the answers, a)–d), below.

1 Who likes Martyn?
2 Who do older viewers like?
3 Who annoys Martyn?
4 Who does Martyn annoy?

a) Editors who ignore positive news do.
b) Older viewers do.
c) Some of his colleagues.
d) Martyn.

Now answer these questions.

1 In which questions is *who* the subject and in which is *who* the object?
2 Do we use the auxiliary verb *do* when the question word is the subject, or when it refers to the object?
3 In answers a) and b) what could replace *do*?

6 Make questions and answers based on the news item below.

❝Last week natives solved the mystery of the missing explorer Dr Grindstone, who disappeared thirty years ago. Their chief discovered his watch in the stomach of an ancient crocodile. They believe the crocodile ate him as he was swimming across the Bonkonko River.❞

Who solved the mystery?
Natives did.

1 ..... ? Dr Grindstone did.
2 When did Dr Grindstone disappear? .....
3 ..... ? Their chief did.
4 Where did they find the watch? .....
5 ..... ? The crocodile did.
6 ..... ? As he was trying to swim across the river.

FOCUS ON STYLE

7 Look at the *News wars* text and find the two sentences that contain this information.

1 Martyn Lewis is forty-six years old; he works as a newsreader.
2 Martyn has got the face of an angel.

How is the structure of sentences 1 and 2 different from those you found in the text? Why do newspapers and broadcasters often modify nouns in this way?

8 Change the parts of the sentences which are in *italics* by modifying the noun.

1 *Janine Murray is a local government official who* runs a hostel for young people.
2 *Rupert, who was the victim of a car crash,* thinks dangerous drivers should be sent to prison.
3 *Felicity Austin, a 39-year-old widow,* is going to re-marry next autumn.
4 *'Chimp' Mitchell, the goalkeeper with long arms,* saves an important penalty.

LISTENING

9 ▭ Listen to a local radio station interviewing passersby about the good news, bad news debate and answer the questions.

1 What does the man think about Martyn Lewis?
2 What example of his own does he give?
3 Who does he blame for all the bad news?

FOCUS ON FUNCTIONS

10 ▭ Listen again and answer these questions.

1 How does the interviewer:
   a) introduce herself?   b) ask a question?
2 How does the man ask for clarification?
3 How does the interviewer ask for an example?
4 What expression is used to give an example?
5 How does the interviewer summarise what she thinks the man has said?
6 Which words does the man use several times in order to 'play for time'?

11 Work in pairs.

Student A: You are the interviewer.
Student B: You are a passerby. Turn to page 128.

When you are ready, role play the interview by following the cues below.

INTERVIEWER	PASSERBY
Explain what you're doing and ask if it's OK to ask his/her opinion.	
	Agree to help.
Ask what he/she thinks about Martyn Lewis's role.	
	Give your opinion.
Ask for an example of what he/she means.	
	Give an example.
Ask for clarification.	
	Clarify.

Say cheese!

GETTING STARTED

1 You are walking along a lonely beach when you recognise a famous film star hiding behind his dark glasses. Do you:

a) ask for his autograph?
b) respect his privacy and ignore him?
c) shout 'say cheese' and take some photographs?
d) do c) *and* sell the photographs to a weekly magazine?

READING

2 Read this introduction and find out how the photograph above launched the career of the man who took it.

Don McCullin is Britain's most distinguished war photographer. He was brought up in Finsbury Park, a rough area in North London. When a policeman died in a gang battle, the press became interested. McCullin, a keen amateur photographer, knew members of the gang and took some photographs to *The Observer* newspaper.

3 Now read the extract on the right.

1 Where is Don at the start of this text?
2 Did the picture editor know Don's work?
3 Had McCullin had contact with the police before?
4 What would have happened if he hadn't found the receipt?
5 Why does Don feel he protected the police?

Taken from *Unreasonable Behaviour* by Don McCullin, Vintage, 1992

DEVELOPING VOCABULARY

4 Guess the meaning of these colloquial words and expressions in the text.

1 the law
2 that broke them up
3 rummaged through
4 nipped out
5 they went all oily
6 a copper harassing me
7 she would have brained them

5 Look at these sentences from the text which have been put into reported speech. Think of what was said, then check your answers with the text.

1 They told me to get in the car.
2 I told them not to park outside my house.
3 He said that he liked the picture and (that) he was going to use it.
4 He asked me if I had taken them.
5 He asked me if I would do some more for him.

Which sentences report:

a) statements?   c) commands?
b) questions?   d) requests?

The picture editor, a man called Cliff Hopkinson looked carefully through my folder, then swung back in his chair and gave me a long inquisitive look.

'Did you take these?' he said at last.

'Yes,' was all I replied.

He said, 'I like this picture and I'm going to use it. Would you do some more for me?'

I left, full of excitement, with a formal commission for more pictures, and a writer by the name of Clancy Sigal was asked to produce the story. Yet Finsbury Park was still to have its say in the matter.

Even as I was leaving the café in Blackstock Road, at the end of a session photographing the boys, I saw the familiar Wolseley waiting. As I approached, the car door opened and I heard the friendly invitation from the law.

'Get in.'

I said, 'No.'

'Get in if you know what's good for you.'

I got in. Always resist the first time, but never take it too far. That was the game around here.

'We've reason to believe that you have been in

6 Answer these questions about reported speech in the past.

1 Grammatically, what follows *say* and *tell*?
2 What usually happens when tenses are reported?
3 How are orders and instructions reported? Include negative orders, e.g. *'Don't park outside my house.'*
4 How are these modals reported?
    will   would   can   may   could   might
5 How are these questions reported?
    a) *'Wh'* questions (*who, what, where*, etc.)
       'Where do you live?' He asked me …
    b) Requests
       'Can you open this?' She asked me …
    c) *'Yes/No'* questions
       'Do you have a pen?' He asked me …

7 Imagine you are Don McCullin telling a friend about the incident. What would you say? Use reported speech.

DISCOVERING LANGUAGE

8 📼 Listen to four sentences taken from the extract. Which sentence is:

a) an offer?   c) a warning?
b) an accusation?   d) an order?

---

that café with a stolen camera.'
    I told them it was not stolen. They asked to see the purchase receipt, which of course I didn't have with me. They suggested a short drive to where I lived to find the receipt, otherwise I'd be heading straight for the police station.
    'Okay,' I said, 'but do me a favour – don't park outside my house. If my mother sees you, you'll be in terrible trouble.'
    That broke them up: 'So your mother is tough, eh?' but they did as I asked. I went into the house, rummaged through my little chest of drawers and found the receipt. When the old lady asked what I was doing I just said that I was tidying up. When I nipped out to show the police they went all oily.
    'Can we drop you back to where we first found you, sir?'
    It was a wonderful moment, refusing a copper's favour and seeing them off. And of course I really had been of assistance to the law. If my mother had come across them harassing me over the camera, there is no question, she would have brained them with the heaviest available ornament.   33

---

9 These sentences all use reporting verbs. Which of the sentences in Exercise 8 are they reporting?

1 They *told* him to get in the car.
2 He *warned* them not to park outside his house.
3 They *offered* to take him back.
4 They *accused* him of stealing a camera.

Which of the reporting verbs follows these grammatical patterns?

a) you … *to do* something
b) you … someone (*not*) *to do* something (2)
c) you … someone + preposition + *doing* something

With the help of a dictionary, find out which patterns these four reporting verbs follow.

order   threaten   congratulate   persuade

10 Rephrase these sentences using each of the reporting verbs above in the past tense.

PAUL: So you passed your exam. Well done Mary!
Paul congratulated Mary on passing her exam.

1 ANNA: Don't touch the switch, Tom. It's dangerous.
2 JANE: You took my book, Sue!
3 CARLOS: I'll help you if you like, Janet.
4 LAUREN: Here you are, Patty. Have a chocolate. Go on, just one. … Good!
5 MIRIAM: You bad boy, David. Stop it or I'll phone your mother.
6 CAROLE: Get in the car at once, Andrew.
7 ANGELA: Put your seat belt on, John, please.

LISTENING

11 📼 Imagine you work for a photographic agency. Listen to the messages which have been left on the answering machine and make notes.

Name of caller	Message
Maggie Page (for Barry)	Has to cancel session Weds– model sick

WRITING

12 Now leave a full message for your boss, where necessary using an appropriate reporting verb. Report the events in the past.

Focus

TOPIC
• News reporting

SKILLS
• Listening: a monologue/news report
• Speaking: reporting

SPEECH PATTERNS
• Making contrasts: stress

Reporting

📠 Documentary

LISTENING

1 BBC news reporter Carole Walker talks about her job. Before you listen, discuss these questions in groups.

1 What do you think an international reporter's job involves? Which aspects of this work would you find enjoyable and which would you find difficult?
2 What kind of personal qualities and strengths do you think an international reporter needs?

2 📼 Now listen and find out why Carole thinks her job is so special.

Carole talks about being in the 'front row' of events which shape history. Exactly what do you think she means by this? Are there any recent historical events where you would have liked a 'front-row' seat?

3 📼 Carole describes the routine of making a news item. Before you listen, put her working routine in order (some activities may occur simultaneously). Then listen to check.

a) She records her voice track.
b) She goes out with the camera crew.
c) She takes the pictures back.
d) She works with an editor.
e) She films.
f) The editor puts the pictures together.

4 Carole talks about the 'art' of reporting. Before you listen, discuss these questions.

1 What main difficulty do you think international reporters face with unhelpful governments?
2 How can a reporter gather news which is balanced and not 'biased'.

📼 **Now listen and find out what she says.**

5 Imagine that this is a trainee reporter speaking to Carole. What advice do you think she would give?

❝ I've got this great story, Carole. If we hurry, it could go out on the six o'clock news. It's all about this man who set fire to his neighbour's car; he just went crazy. It seems as though he did it for no reason. The owner told me everything. ❞

6 🖭 **Listen to Carole's report about the crash of a cargo plane close to Amsterdam's Schiphol airport. Answer the questions and complete the notes.**

1 Where was the flight recorder?
2 Why did the fire keep going for such a long time?
3 Complete these details about the flight.

Flight number	LY 1862
Duration of flight	.....
Altitude	.....
Problem	.....

At first the authorities thought ..... had died, but then they changed the number to .....
Why? .....

7 Work in pairs. Discuss these questions.

1 How do you think Carole applied her reporting approach, described in Exercise 4, to the Amsterdam air crash story?
2 How many different people do you think she had to interview?

SPEECH PATTERNS

8 🖭 **Listen again to this part of Carole's report. Which of the two numbers does she stress and why?**

❝ The Mayor gave a press conference and we asked why, for example, initially the death toll had been put in excess of 200, it was later revised to about 80.❞

SPEAKING

9 Work in groups of four.

A local TV station is reporting an incident where a dog has attacked two children. The children are recovering in hospital. The dog, a family pet, has been destroyed by the authorities.

Student A: You are Reporter 1. Interview the postman.
Student B: You are Reporter 2. Interview the neighbour.
Ask *what* happened and *why* they think it happened. Find out about the dog and the children who were attacked. Then compare your notes with the other reporter.

Student C: You are the postman who rescued the children. You saw the dog attack the children. You think it was terrible. The children were playing on their bicycles when the dog attacked without warning. You think the dog was vicious and can't understand why people are allowed to keep such dangerous animals. The same dog attacked you last year. You think the dog escaped from the garden.

Student D: You are the neighbour. You saw what happened but you don't think that it was the dog's fault. The children always used to tease the dog by throwing stones at it and pulling its tail. You think the children provoked the dog and that their mother should have told them to keep away from it.

10 Now work as a group of four and create a short news item about the incident.

Write the scripts for the reporters. Follow the advice Carole gave in the interview:

- STAND BACK
- BE SCEPTICAL
- CHECK THE FACTS
- FIND OUT THE OTHER SIDE OF THE STORY
- DON'T BELIEVE EVERYTHING
- APPROACH EVERYONE

REPORTER 1

Introduce the story from the studio. Give the background to the story. Begin like this:
'Good evening. Here is the local news. Two children are in hospital after being attacked by a family pet. ...'
Go on to say:
a) when the attack happened.
b) how they were rescued.
c) what has happened to the dog.
End your presentation like this:
'We are now going over to the scene of the attack.'

REPORTER 2

Give a report from where the incident actually happened. Begin like this:
'I am standing outside the garden where the attack took place ...'
Go on to:
a) say what the children were doing when it happened.
b) include a *short* live interview with the postman and the neighbour.

Grammar reference

GRAMMAR

1 Wh- pronouns in questions

- When the pronoun *who* is the subject of a sentence, the structure is:
  Who + verb (+ object)
  EXAMPLES: *Who lives next door?*
  Who shot the President?
- When *who* is the object of the sentence, the structure is often:
  Who + auxiliary verb *do* + subject + verb
  EXAMPLES: *Who did they see?*
  Who does he want to speak to?

2 Reported speech

- We use reported speech to refer to a statement or question that we or another person made earlier.
  Direct: *'We've visited the Parthenon.'*
  Reported: *They said they had visited the Parthenon.*
- When we change sentences from direct to reported speech, the pronouns, tense and adverbs of place and time may all change.
  EXAMPLE: *'I'll see you here tomorrow at five o'clock.'*
  She said she would see him there the next day at five o'clock.
- Notice, however, that the tense of the verb does NOT change:
  a) if the verb in direct speech is already in the past perfect or past perfect progressive tense and cannot be changed.
     EXAMPLE: *'I'd completely forgotten.'*
     He said he had completely forgotten.
  b) with modals *would, could, should* and *might*.
- Remember also that it is sometimes not logical to change the time and place adverbials, if the reporter is speaking on the same day or in the same place as the original speaker.
  EXAMPLE: *'I'll see him here tomorrow.'*
  She said she would see you here tomorrow.

3 Common reporting verbs

- The most common reporting verbs are *say* and *tell*. The structure is:
  say (that) + reported statement
  tell someone (that) + reported statement
  EXAMPLES: *I said (that) I agreed.*
  I told her (that) I agreed.
  Notice that *say* is not followed by an indirect object.

4 Reported requests and orders

- The verbs *ask* and *tell* are used to report requests and orders. The structure is:
  ask/tell + indirect object + *(not) to* + infinitive
  EXAMPLES: *He asked me to help him.* (request)
  He told me to sit down and be quiet. (order)

5 Reported questions

- When we report a *Yes/No* question, the reporting verb is followed by *if* or *whether*.
  EXAMPLE: *'Do you live in London?'*
  He asked her if/whether she lived in London.
- When we report *wh-* questions, we repeat the question word.
  EXAMPLE: *'Where do you live?'*
  He asked her where she lived. (NOT *He asked her where she did live.*)

6 Other reporting verbs

- There are many other reporting verbs. They use different grammatical patterns, with or without a direct object, and end with an *-ing* form or infinitive:

VERB	OBJECT	PREPOSITION	
accuse	someone	of	doing something
congratulate	someone	on	doing something
apologise	—	for	doing something
admit	—	(to)	doing something
suggest	—	—	doing something

VERB	OBJECT	TO + INFINITIVE
advise persuade remind warn	someone	(not) to do something
offer promise refuse threaten	—	to do something

- These verbs often report the general idea of what someone said rather than repeating the exact words.
  EXAMPLES: *'I'm sorry I'm late.'* → *He apologised for being late.*
  'Let's go swimming.' → *She suggested going swimming.*
  'If I were you, I'd destroy the letter.' → *He advised her to destroy the letter.*

Progress check Units 8–9

1 Make these sentences passive. Only include *by* **plus an agent if this information is useful.**

1 The wind blew down five trees in yesterday's storm.
2 People in Britain eat a lot of Indian food.
3 You can't copy banknotes easily.
4 Gérard Depardieu plays the main character in *Cyrano*.
5 They're questioning three people about the theft of a Van Gogh from the National Gallery.
6 Someone has discovered an unexplored tunnel inside the Great Pyramid.
7 Barcelona beat Arsenal four goals to nil.
8 Children have caused the damage to the school.

2 Put the words into the correct order to make passive sentences.

1 this bill to week ought be our telephone paid
2 was this microwave think a meal do cooked you in?
3 flat at the moment redecorated our being is
4 every exercised dog be a day needs large to

3 Complete the dialogue with an appropriate *will* **or** *going to* **form of the verb in brackets.**

DAVE: Right! I've decided I've got to get fit! From now on I ¹..... (go) jogging when I get home from work. No more sitting in front of the television.
DIANE: Oh, I've heard that before. Last year you ²..... (join) a keep-fit class, but you did nothing about it. Knowing you, I expect you ³..... (go) once or twice and then give up. And anyway, who ⁴..... (help) me with the dinner while you're out jogging?
DAVE: Don't worry. I ⁵..... (do) my share of the cooking. You ⁶..... (see).
DIANE: Did you get some milk?
DAVE: Oh, I'm sorry. I ⁷..... (stop) and buy some on the way home!

4 Write questions about Tutankhamen and his tomb to match the following answers. Use all the words in brackets.

1 He was a pharaoh in Ancient Egypt. (who)
2 He died in 1352 BC, when he had ruled for less than ten years. (when)
3 It is in the Valley of the Kings at Thebes. (where)
4 It was discovered in 1922. (when)
5 The archaeologists Lord Carnarvon and Howard Carter. (who)
6 They found Tutankhamen's solid gold coffin and many other magnificent works of art. (what)

5 Complete the sentences, using the correct form of these reporting verbs: *accuse, ask, offer, persuade, warn.* **Then rewrite each sentence in direct speech.**

1 He ..... to go with her to the airport.
2 She ..... me of reading her diary.
3 My friend ..... me to help her with her essay.
4 I ..... him not to use the car because the brakes needed checking.
5 He ..... me whether I had ever been skiing.

6 Complete the sentences by rearranging the letters to form a proper word.

1 A person who can't walk or has a physical handicap is ..... (lidaesdb).
2 A ..... (aomyr) is an elected official who represents a town or city.
3 A ..... (rsawrdneee) is a TV or radio journalist who tells you about the day's important events.
4 A ..... (kccotpikpe) is a kind of thief who steals money from your clothes without you noticing.
5 A ..... (ldavna) often destroys or damages property just for fun.

10 *The older the better*

Focus

TOPIC
• Old and new

GRAMMAR
• Zero, first, second and third conditionals

FUNCTIONS
• Stating preferences

SKILLS
• Listening: a conversation

SPEECH PATTERNS
• Showing enthusiasm: stress

Traditional values

GETTING STARTED

1 Look at the pairs of objects and discuss which ones you prefer.

LISTENING

2 📼 Listen to Margaret Green talking about the tastes of British people. What does she say about:

a) houses?　　c) cars?
b) furniture?　d) clothes and fashion?

FOCUS ON FUNCTIONS

3 Study these sentences.
a) British people **prefer** old things to new things.
b) They**'d rather** have antique furniture than something modern.

1 Which sentence describes preferences in general?
2 Which sentence is used to make a specific choice between two things?
3 Grammatically, what follows *prefer* and *would rather*?

⟳ COMPARING CULTURES

4 Compare what Margaret said about Britain with tastes in your own country.

🖻 Documentary

5 Read about Christie's.

Christie's is a London auction house which was founded in 1776. Mark Poltimore specialises in nineteenth-century paintings at Christie's. He is going to value this painting.

Describe the painting of Venice in detail and say what you think of it.

LISTENING

6 Before you listen, work in pairs and discuss these questions.

1 What nationalities might like the painting?
2 If you had the money, how much would you bid for it at auction?

7 Listen to Mark assessing the painting. Complete the details and answer the questions.

❝Well, the first impression is wonderful. Erm, it's by this artist called Rubens [1]..... who's an [2]..... artist and, I think he was born in the [3]..... and he died in [4]..... in [5]..... . He specialised really on these sort of architectural views and here we have I think a beautiful view of [6]..... and I have to say it is one of the nicest I've seen for a long time.❞

1 What in particular does Mark like about the painting?
2 Who does *he* think might want to buy it?
3 What is its maximum and minimum value?

SPEECH PATTERNS

8 Look at the text in Exercise 7. Which words show Mark's enthusiasm? Listen again to what he says and underline the words he stresses.

9 Imagine you are an auctioneer in 200 years time. Choose an object in your classroom and speak enthusiastically about it as though it were an antique.

LISTENING

10 Mark explains how he knows the painting is genuine. Listen and answer the questions.

1 What is special about the painting?
2 What can you see through a magnifying glass?
3 What would the painting have been worth if there had been a problem with it? Write down Mark's exact words.
 'If it .... considerably less.'
4 Victoria asks: *What's the next step?* Write down Mark's exact words.
 'Well, if you .... include it in our next important sale.'
5 If she decides to sell, what will it cost her?

11 Listen to Mark talking about the actual auction.

1 What happens if the auction moves too slowly?
2 Write down Mark's exact words.
 'If it .... bored.'
3 How many lots (items) does he sell in an hour?

12 Listen to the final part of the interview.

1 What advice does Mark give people who may own something of value?
2 Why does he say that people must come in? Write down his exact words.
 'But you must come in because if you .... the picture on the wall or in the attic is valuable.'

REVIEWING LANGUAGE

13 Look at the four sentences you wrote down with Mark's exact words.

1 Which sentence describes:
 a) an imaginary past situation which is contrary to known facts?
 b) an established fact, something that is always true?
 c) a future event which is likely to happen?
 d) a possible result of a condition which can easily be met?
2 Identify the conditional sentences. Which is a zero conditional? Why is it used?

14 Comment on and expand these situations, using an appropriate conditional.

1 Your friend Tony didn't have a proper valuation for a painting he sold and lost a lot of money.
 If you'd had a valuation, you might not have sold the painting. If you .....
2 Your friend Marie wants to sell a painting privately. You think she'll make more money if she takes it to an auctioneer. You think this is unlikely.
 If you .....
3 People who invest in paintings make a lot of money. You think it is a well-known fact.
 If you .....
4 Stop a friend from cleaning an old painting with petrol. You think he'll ruin it.
 If you .....

Objects of desire

GETTING STARTED

1 Look at the pictures of souvenirs someone has collected from trips abroad. What are they? Where do they come from?

2 Work in pairs. What kind of souvenirs do you like to collect? What typical souvenirs do visitors to your country buy?

READING

3 Look at the photograph of some medieval treasure and discuss this question.

What do you think the connection could be between these things?

a king   a mine in Germany   three million dollars
an American soldier

Now read the text and find out.

4 Find or suggest answers to these questions.

1 How were Joe Meador's souvenirs different from those of most soldiers?
2 How do we know that the treasure was from a superstitious age?
3 Why were the items put down a mine?
4 Why do you think the Americans gave up their investigation?
5 Why did such a long time pass between the first and second investigations?
6 Why do you think Meador left the treasure to his brother and sister?

DEVELOPING VOCABULARY

5 Find adjectives in the text which deal with value or the absence of value.

6 Complete these sentences with the adjectives you found.

1 This painting is of such great value it is really ..... .
2 That chair should be quite ..... , it is over two hundred years old.
3 What they thought was gold turned out to be a ..... piece of metal.
4 The visit to the gallery wasn't a waste of time at all – I found it extremely ..... .
5 Gold, silver and platinum are all ..... metals.

Focus

TOPIC
• Valuable objects

GRAMMAR
• Adjective order
• Noun phrases

SKILLS
• Reading: a newspaper article
• Speaking: a discussion/ describing an object
• Listening: a description of an object
• Writing: a description of an object

VOCABULARY DEVELOPMENT
• Adjectives related to value

SPEAKING

7 Discuss these questions which consider the moral dimension.

1 Was it right that Meador's heirs received so much money?
2 In war, is it fair for soldiers to take the property of the people they conquer?
3 What would happen if everything that was lost in this way was returned? What national treasures would your country lose or gain?

THE QUEDLINBURG TREASURE

When US soldier Lieutenant Joe Meador left Germany at the end of the Second World War, he went home with something more valuable than memories. Instead of a helmet or a worthless souvenir he returned with some priceless medieval treasure. The items included a small early tenth-century chest made of gold, silver and ivory and precious jewels, some wonderful rare manuscripts and a unique golden comb which it was once believed could comb away your sins!

The chest was also of great historical importance as it showed King Heinrich I of Saxony, Germany's first elected king. The treasures had been kept in the church of Quedlinburg, but were hidden down a mine during the war.

DISCOVERING LANGUAGE

8 Look at this phrase from the text.

a small early tenth-century chest

1 Does the adjective of size or age come first?
In English, adjectives tend to follow this order:
opinion, size/shape, age, colour, origin, material + NOUN

2 Which of the categories do these adjectives belong to?
silver   ancient   priceless   long   rectangular   purple
wonderful   Turkish   small   silk   Egyptian   jade   oval
huge   early tenth-century   golden   English   wooden

3 Adjectives which describe the purpose of an object always go
directly before the noun, e.g. *A priceless steel **hunting** gun.*

4 It can appear ugly to have too many adjectives before the noun.
We can avoid it like this:
a) noun + *with* + e.g. *jewels*
b) noun + *made of/from* material: noun + country of origin
c) noun + clause, e.g. *... which was beautiful*

When the American forces occupied the city, Meador was put in charge of guarding the mine. The treasure mysteriously disappeared. The American authorities looking into the matter gave up their investigation when they withdrew and the city became part of communist East Germany. The new rulers had little interest in retrieving the treasure.

Following the fall of the communist regime, the united country was keen to find out what had happened to it. Their search led them to Meador who had died in 1980. In his will he had left the treasure to his brother and sister. Delicate negotiations in London were extremely worthwhile for his heirs, who pocketed three million dollars in exchange for the treasure. Before it left for Germany, the Dallas Museum of Art was allowed to show the Meador collection for seven weeks. More than 30,000 people came to view it. ■

9 Write sentences from the information below which follow the rules of adjective order.

This wedding dress is from France. It is extremely beautiful. It is made of silk.
It's a beautiful silk wedding dress from France.
This is a beautiful French wedding dress made of silk.

1 This statue is from China. It is small and the workmanship is wonderful. It is made of jade.
2 This spear comes from Africa. It was used for hunting. It is made of hard wood and has beautiful carving on it.
3 This is a manuscript. It is priceless. It is written in Arabic. It is extremely rare.
4 It is a bracelet. It is made of gold. It is from Ancient Egypt.

LISTENING

10 ▭ Natacha Tessier is talking about a Russian samovar. Listen and make notes about the following.

1 What it is and how long the family has had it.
2 The material it is made of.
3 Anything interesting about its manufacture.
4 Its description.
5 Its importance to her.
6 What it was used for and how it was used.

SPEAKING

11 Work in pairs or groups. Describe an object that belongs to you or your family.

WRITING

12 Write a short description of the object.

Describing a person

SPEAKING

1 At what age do you think people become old?

2 Look at these photographs and decide what is special about the people in them.

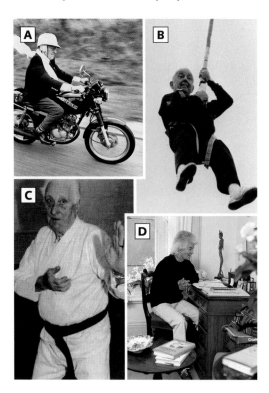

LISTENING

3 🔲 Listen and find out who the people are and what they have done.

🔄 COMPARING CULTURES

4 Read and discuss the following.
In Britain, people generally retire at 65. Most elderly people live on their own and it is comparatively unusual for them to live with sons or daughters. It is common for them to go into old people's homes when they are no longer capable of looking after themselves. What is the situation in your own country?

READING

5 Work in pairs. Each read one text.
Which portrait best matches the person in the text?
Describe one of the portraits to your partner. Can they choose the correct one?

1

Rose stared. He was not much older than she. Tall, thin, dressed in clothes she had only seen worn by French workmen, baggy cotton trousers in faded blue, a baggy jacket to match over a dark flannel shirt, collarless, fastened at the neck with a bone stud. He had thick, almost black hair worn rather longer than most people, a thin eager face, longish nose, wide mouth and black intelligent eyes.

2

Madame Tarasova shook hands with Cosmo as he turned back into the room.

'So you too are a player of backgammon, my national game.'

'No, but I'd like to learn,' said Cosmo looking down at Madame Tarasova who, less than five feet tall, looked up at him. She was tiny, with miniature hands and feet, greying hair pulled back severely in a bun, a paper-pale skin, large black eyes and an enormous arrogantly hooked nose above a sweet-tempered mouth. She looked considerably older than her twenty-nine years.

as we arrived at the house.

We pushed back the gate and stepped into the garden. A glorious chestnut tree in full leaf shaded much of it, yet parts were dappled with patches of intense sunlight which bleached the pink hydrangeas in the borders. By the strip of earth above the wine cellar stood her grandfather: a man of eighty-four years, his face frozen in concentration, his surgeon's fingers training the branches of a newly-planted cherry tree. Despite the heat he wore grey flannel trousers, two cardigans, a brightly coloured cravat and a large misshapen sun hat. His neck sticking out from the layers of clothing was like a tortoise's emerging from its shell. He heard us approach and turned towards us. As he removed his hat to embrace my fiancée, I saw his head was bald except for a few wisps of baby fine grey hair. His skin was smooth and waxen and his head dominated by a large and surprisingly line-free forehead. He gripped my hand and gave me a smile full of the charm of a benign infant. Yet his blue eyes, now milky with age, revealed a keen and appraising intelligence. Here was the test I had to pass.

58

DEVELOPING VOCABULARY

6 Now read both texts quickly and answer these questions.

1 Which adjectives in Text 1 mean:
   a) loose/opposite of tight?
   b) having lost its original brightness?
   c) without a collar?
   d) fairly long?

2 How could you say that something was:
   a) fairly short?
   b) fairly cheap?
   c) fairly smart?
   d) fairly old?
   Can we use -ish with words like beautiful, tired or interesting?

3 In Text 2, which words have the idea of smallness and largeness?

4 Which colour is used as a verb? What does it mean?

5 Madame Tarasova's skin was as pale as paper; how does the author say this? How would you say:
   a) the carpet was as red as blood?
   b) her eyes were as cold as ice?
   c) her hair was as black as jet?

FOCUS ON STYLE

7 Read Text 2 again quickly and discuss these questions.

What contradiction is there between Madame Tarasova's nose and her mouth; and between her looks and her age? How does this make the description more interesting?

Text 1 on page 84 is from *Not that sort of girl* by Mary Wesley, Black Swan, 1988. Text 2 is from *A sensible life* by Mary Wesley, Bantam Press, 1990.

READING

8 You are going to write a description of an older person. First, read the text above and answer these questions.

1 What time of year was it?
2 What was the grandfather doing when they arrived?
3 How was he dressed?
4 What did he remind the writer of?
5 What was special about his face?

9 Now answer these questions.

1 How hot was it? What effect did the sun have?
2 What kind of person would plant a cherry tree at the age of eighty-four?
3 What contradictions are there in the text?
4 How did he greet the writer; what clue did this give about his personality?
5 What does the writer mean by the final line?

WRITING

10 Think of the first time you met somebody and the initial impression that you had of them. Make notes under these headings.

1 The location: where you first met the person.
2 When you first saw them./What they were doing.
3 What they were wearing.
4 Physical description: dress, build, face, skin, eyes.
5 Personality/character.
6 Anything contradictory/surprising.

11 Using the text as a guide, write a description of a person based on a first meeting.

Grammar reference

1 Zero conditional sentences

- We use the zero conditional to talk about established facts and situations that are always or usually true.
  EXAMPLES: *If you heat butter, it melts quickly.*
  If I drink coffee, I get a headache.
  We always go out on Sundays unless the weather is bad.

  Notice the use of the pronoun *you* in the first example to mean 'people in general, including you and me'.

FORM

- The standard form of the zero conditional is:
  If + present tense clause + present tense clause
  The present progressive tense is sometimes used.
  EXAMPLE: *If John **is working**, I **try** not to disturb him.*

- As with other conditional sentences, either the *if* clause or the consequence clause can come first. When the consequence clause comes first, there is usually no comma between the clauses.
  EXAMPLE: *Life is more fun if you have a positive attitude.*

- *If* in zero conditional sentences can usually be replaced by *when*.
  EXAMPLE: *When John **is working**, I **try** to be quiet.*
  See Grammar reference Unit 7 for notes on the first, second and third conditionals.

2 Order of adjectives

- When we use two or more adjectives before a noun, we usually (but not always) put them in a certain order:
  size/length – shape/width – age – colour – origin – material
  EXAMPLES: *a tall elegant French actress*
  a tiny blue Chinese porcelain vase

- Some adjectives and nouns are so often used together, however, that we do not apply this rule.
  Compare: *Italian white wine*
  a white Italian car

- Some adjectives are 'opinion' adjectives, which we use to say what we personally think of someone or something. They include:
  nice, lovely, pretty, beautiful, delicious, ugly, horrible, disgusting
  Opinion adjectives usually come before adjectives of fact.
  EXAMPLES: *a beautiful old Georgian house*
  a lovely young girl
  a box of delicious Belgian chocolates.

- Although long lists of adjectives are sometimes used before nouns, we often avoid them by putting some of the information after the noun instead.
  EXAMPLES: *horrible hard seats made of shiny purple plastic*
  a richly decorated ceremonial sword from Tunisia

- When there are several adjectives after a verb, we usually put *and* before the last one and commas between the others.
  EXAMPLES: *His hair was long, dark and curly.*
  The river was deep, dark, fast-flowing and dangerous.

- The adjectives *glad*, *well*, *ill* and *ready* are unusual because we cannot usually put them before a noun.
  EXAMPLES: *The doctor is ready.* (But NOT *the ready doctor*)
  The woman is ill. (But *the sick woman* NOT *the ill woman*.)

Talkback

Turtles or tourists?

1 Read this introduction.

Prectius is a small Mediterranean island. North Prectius is a highly developed tourist area and a popular destination for package tours from northern Europe. A new road means that the west coast of the island around the village of St Geronimo, until now untouched by tourism, can now be developed.

2 Read the notes about St Geronimo and identify what the symbols on the map refer to.

> **Fact-file: St Geronimo**
> **Location:** Small fishing village on west coast of island of Prectius, Eastern Mediterranean.
> **Communications:** Poor – weekly ferry to St Nicholas. Next year new coast road will link St Geronimo to international airport.
> **Population:** 650. Most young people emigrate.
> **Local economy:** Fishing and agriculture.
> **Culture:** Many folk traditions. Ruins of ancient amphitheatre.

3 You are going to read a short passage about a problem facing Prectius. Before you read, make connections between the pictures and try to predict what the article will be about.

Turtles versus tourists

AROUND a fifth of all green turtles are hatched on the western shores of Prectius. Every year, each female turtle buries about 250 eggs in the sand, but only one in a thousand becomes an adult. In other parts of the Mediterranean, turtles are threatened with extinction because of increased pollution. If the development goes ahead, newly-hatched turtles could be confused by the bright lights and be led inland. Beach umbrellas driven into the sand could kill many more. Environmentalists believe that the beach should be a turtle reserve. Alternatively, development could be restricted to just one part of the beach. However, this part of the island is poor and perfect for tourist development. Within three years St Geronimo could be a thriving resort, but all that may be left of the turtles could be the green plastic souvenirs.

4 Discuss what should happen to St Geronimo. Work in two groups.

Group A: List the advantages of tourist development.
Group B: List the disadvantages of tourist development.

Think about traditional life as well as the environment.

Now work in pairs, one student from each of the groups, and decide whether the development should go ahead or not.

11 *Against the odds*

Focus

TOPIC
• Disabled person's achievements

GRAMMAR
• Infinitives and -*ing* forms

SKILLS
• Listening: a monologue
• Reading: a newspaper article

VOCABULARY DEVELOPMENT
• Noun suffixes

Turning points

GETTING STARTED

1 Identify the sports in the pictures.

1 Which is the most dangerous/exciting?
2 Have you ever done any of them?
3 What kind of person do you need to be to participate in them?

🔲 Documentary

" I'm a scuba diver. I take a yearly trip to Bonayre in the Netherland Antilles to scuba dive. "

LISTENING

2 Before you listen, discuss the following.
Mike Haynes does all three sports in the pictures above, but he is not an ordinary sportsman. Can you guess why?

3 🔲 Listen to Mike and find out what is different about him.
Which word does Mike use as the opposite of *disabled*?

4 🔲 Mike now works with other disabled people. Listen and answer the questions.

1 What is the purpose of St David's?
2 How are wheelchair sports classified?
3 How does Mike help the patients who come to St David's?
4 According to Mike, what does strength give to disabled people?

DEVELOPING VOCABULARY

5 Look at these nouns from the interview. Notice they all have different suffixes.
recreat*ion*   disabili*ty*   fit*ness*   independ*ence*

Make nouns from the following verbs and adjectives. List them according to the suffixes above. Use a dictionary to help you if necessary.
operate   depressed   opportune   different   inform   able   conform   educate   happy   exist

Add any other nouns you know which have the same endings.

READING

6 Read this newspaper article about Mike and answer as many of the questions as you can.

1 How old was Mike at the time of the incident?
2 What was the cause of the incident?
3 Where did it happen?
4 What did Mike say to the other man?
5 How many shots were fired?
6 In which part of the body was Mike hit?
7 When did Mike realise he was paralysed?
8 What happened to the gunman?

SHOOTING VICTIM IN SERIOUS CONDITION

A 20-YEAR-OLD Austin man remained in a serious condition Sunday night with a bullet wound in the head after an argument with a motorist in South Austin.

Michael Haynes, 2201 Village Way Drive, may have been paralysed by the gunshot wound, police said.

Police said Haynes was driving along South Congress Avenue about 11.45 p.m. Saturday when he apparently exchanged words with another driver.

Haynes and the other person pulled into the parking lot of the Utotem convenience store at 4619 S. Congress Ave. and continued to argue. The other person then fired two shots, one of which struck Haynes in the back of the head. The other shot missed.

No arrests have been made, police said.

LISTENING

7 Listen to Mike's account of the incident. Answer any remaining questions above. Are there any differences between the two accounts?

8 After Mike was shot, he went through a very difficult period in his life. Listen to him talking about it and answer the questions.

1 How easy was it for Mike to find help and information after his injury? What kind of problems did he have?
2 Why does Mike say he wants new patients at St David's to view him as a resource?
3 How does he show new arrivals what possibilities exist for them?

✪ COMPARING CULTURES

9 Work in pairs and discuss these questions.

What provision is available for disabled people in your country? What facilities are there to help them with their disabilities?

REVIEWING LANGUAGE

10 Read what someone said about Mike:

❛ His life is so impressive because it shows how he has **managed to come** to terms with his disability. Since being shot he has **succeeded in building** a new life. ❜

1 Look at the parts of the sentences in **bold** type. How are the two structures different?
2 Which of the verbs below are followed by:
a) the infinitive, e.g. *manage to do?*
b) the *-ing* form, e.g. *succeed in doing?*
Use your dictionary to help you.
refuse   look forward to   mind   want   dare   hope   involve   seem   give up   risk   promise   avoid   plan

11 Change the verbs below into the infinitive or the *-ing* form. Then complete the sentences.

1 I wouldn't dare (go) scuba diving if I were disabled; it sounds …
2 I don't know what is wrong with young people; on the bus the other day one refused (give) his seat to …
3 Mike always looks forward to (go) on holiday each year as …
4 Disabled people avoid (visit) buildings with stairs and …
5 Don't risk (break) your neck; go down the blue slope instead …
6 Susan seems (be) much happier since she attended St David's and …
7 Physiotherapy often involves (do) lots of painful …
8 She promised (write) every month when she left the centre and …

12 Work in pairs. Take turns to ask and answer these questions.

1 Would you ever dare to do a parachute jump?
2 Would you risk breaking an arm or a leg in a sport?
3 Have you given up playing a sport? If yes, why did you stop?
4 Have you ever managed to win a sporting competition? If yes, what was it?
5 How much do you mind losing a game or match?
6 Are there any sports or activities you would refuse to play or watch?

13 Choose one of the questions and write a short paragraph about it.

Fighting back

Focus

TOPIC
• Fighting disease

GRAMMAR
• Phrasal verbs

FUNCTIONS
• Hesitating

SKILLS
• Reading: an article
• Speaking: a discussion
• Listening: a discussion

GETTING STARTED

1 Look at the questionnaire about life expectancy and answer the questions.

> ### QUESTIONNAIRE
>
> Compared with the past, people are supposed to be living longer, but ... how long have we got?
>
> 1 World life expectancy is ..... years.
>   a) 46.3   c) 63.9
>   b) 54.7   d) 71.2
>
> 2 Forty years ago world life expectancy was ..... years.
>   a) 27.5   c) 47.5
>   b) 37.5   d) 57.5
>
> 3 The country with the highest life expectancy is:
>   a) Japan.
>   b) Sweden.
>   c) Tibet.
>   d) Switzerland.
>
> 4 The country with the most doctors per head of population is:
>   a) USA.
>   b) Britain.
>   c) Italy.
>   d) China.

What do you think is the *most* important factor in people living longer?

the conquest of disease
better hygiene
new medical technology

READING

2 Read the text and find out what is so special about the young woman in the photograph. Study the meanings of the words in **bold** type given in the glossary.

AGAINST THE ODDS

The Ayalas were an ordinary American family just like millions of others: mom, dad, two kids; a boy and a girl. Until, that is, daughter Anissa was diagnosed as suffering from a kind of leukemia (cancer of the blood).

Her parents soon learned the dreadful truth: the precious child they had *brought up* was under sentence of death. Leukemia claims its victims within five years without a successful bone marrow transplant. At this point Anissa's best bet was her brother Airon, but his marrow proved incompatible. Next, the Ayalas launched an unsuccessful nationwide search for a donor. Time was *running out* .

Anissa's final hope was a child who did not, as yet, exist. Earlier the father Abe had had an operation so there would be no more children. He had it reversed in a procedure which usually only has a 40 per cent success rate. At the age of 43 his wife became pregnant and the family waited, knowing that the odds against the new arrival being compatible were three to one. The gamble succeeded and a daughter with suitable marrow was born.

After a fourteen-month wait, doctors were ready to perform the vital operation. In just twenty minutes at LA's City of Hope hospital they removed a cupful of healthy bone marrow from the infant. The life-giving substance was then dripped into the veins of her elder sister. Even then, success was not guaranteed. Anissa had a 70 per cent chance of success. Fortunately, it succeeded and Anissa slowly *got over* her ordeal to make a full recovery. A year later, in June 1992, she married her sweetheart Bryan Epinosa and they *look forward to* a long life together.

> GLOSSARY
> **bone marrow:** the substance in our bones responsible for producing healthy blood cells.
> **(in)compatible:** if two things are compatible it means that they work well together. (If they are incompatible, they are unsuitable and can't work together.)
> **donor:** someone who gives blood or an organ to a person who needs it.
> **transplant:** to take from the body of one person and give it to another.

3 Find all the words and phrases in the text which can be used to describe risks and probabilities.

4 Look at the title of the article. What do you think the 'odds' (probabilities) were *against* a successful result?

1 Were they: 10 to 1; 20 to 1; 50 to 1; 100 to 1?
2 Which figure gives the best indication? Be ready to explain your answer.

5 In the article, which of the phrasal verbs in *italics* means the following.

1 to come to an end   3 to recover
2 to anticipate with pleasure   4 to raise/educate

DISCOVERING LANGUAGE

6 Phrasal verbs consist of a verb followed by a particle (either a preposition or an adverb). There are four main types of phrasal verb.

1 Type 1 phrasal verbs can't have an object. These are called **intransitive** verbs.
  A *Their money ran out.* (correct)
  B *Their money ran out it.* (wrong – we can't add an object)

The other three types of phrasal verb take an object. These are called *transitive* verbs.

2 Look at these sentences which use the Type 2 phrasal verb *bring up.*
  C *They brought Anissa up.* (correct)
  D *They brought her up.* (correct)
  E *They brought up Anissa.* (correct)
  F *They brought up her.* (wrong)
  Can you work out a rule? Where is it possible to put the noun, i.e. *Anissa?* If we use an object pronoun, i.e. *her,* where must it go? Is it possible to put an object, or object pronoun, between the verb and the particle? Note: This is called a **separable** verb.

3 Look at these sentences which use the Type 3 phrasal verb *get over.*
  G *She got over the illness.* (correct)
  H *She got over it.* (correct)
  I *She got the illness/it over.* (wrong)
  Is it possible to put an object or object pronoun between the verb and the particle? Note: This is called an **inseparable** verb.

4 Type 4 phrasal verbs consist of a verb and two particles, e.g. *look forward to.* They are always followed by an object and *cannot* be separated.

7 Now look at these dictionary entries. How do they tell us the grammar of the phrasal verbs?

> **bring** sbdy./sthg. **up** *v adv* [T] to educate and care for in the family until grown up: *to bring up children*

> **get over** sthg. *v prep* [T] to return to one's normal state of health, happiness, etc. after a bad experience of or with: *to get over an illness/She can't get over the death of her husband.*

> **look forward to** sthg. *v adv prep* [T+*v-ing*] to expect to enjoy (something that is going to happen).

> **run out** *v adv* [I] to come to an end, or have no more: *Have you nearly finished? Time is running out.*

I = intransitive   T = transitive

8 Work in pairs. Use a monolingual English dictionary and find the meanings and types of the phrasal verbs below. Look up three verbs each.

look after   look up to   fall out   set off
put up with   turn up

LISTENING

9 📼 Listen to three friends, Carmen, Baz and Delia, discussing the Ayalas' situation.

1 What justifications do they give for the Ayalas' actions?
2 What criticisms do they make?

FOCUS ON FUNCTIONS

10 📼 Listen again. Answer these questions.

1 The Ayalas' situation is a very difficult topic to discuss, which means that all three sometimes pause to give themselves time to think. What 'sounds' do they make when they hesitate?
2 What expressions do they use to give themselves some thinking time?

SPEAKING

11 Work in groups of three and continue the conversation. Use the questions below to help you and use some of the ways of hesitating which you have heard in Exercise 10.

1 Were the parents right to have another child to save the life of their eldest daughter?
2 How will baby Marissa feel when she is old enough to understand why she was born?
3 Is medical science making people more or less moral?

An advertisement

DEVELOPING VOCABULARY

1 Use your dictionaries to find out the answers to these questions.

1 What's the difference between *advertising* and *publicity*?
2 What is the stress and pronunciation of these words?
 advertise advertisement advertising
 publicity publicise
3 What's the difference between *mercy*, *misery* and *charity*?
4 What's the difference between *human* and *humane*?
5 When would you want to find a *patron*, *donor* or a *sponsor*? What other nouns can you make from these words?

☝ COMPARING CULTURES

2 Work in pairs and discuss the following.

1 In your country, who takes the most responsibility for the disabled and the elderly? Is it the state, families, religious groups, private charities?
2 In Britain, people talk about 'compassion fatigue'. If you have 'compassion fatigue' it means you are tired of being asked to help or donate to charity, i.e. people get fed up with being asked to give money. What is it like in your country?
3 A common English expression is 'charity begins at home'. What do you think it means? How far do you agree with this sentiment?
4 How many images of misery and suffering do you see on TV in your country? Do these images make us hard and uncaring?

Focus

TOPIC
• Charities

SKILLS
• Reading: an advertisement
• Writing: improving a text/an advertisement
• Speaking: planning an advertising campaign

STYLE
• Devices to evoke sympathy

VOCABULARY DEVELOPMENT
• Easily confused words

We're pulling at

Imagine being at the height of your powers.
Imagine fingers that effortlessly move across the strings or keyboard.
Imagine the applause of a packed concert hall.

NO MORE ENCORES

Now, imagine having fingers that no longer do what is required of them. You sit by the phone waiting for the call that never comes. You worry about the pile of unpaid bills. Imagine, after years of creating joy for others, the loneliness and poverty of old age. Imagine the loss of an entire way of life.

Symphony: when

READING

3 Look at this advertisement for a charity.
What kind of charity is the advertisement for? How effective do you think the advert is?

FOCUS ON STYLE

4 Now answer these questions.

1 How does the advertisement help us to identify with the people it is trying to help?
2 What time contrast does the advertisement use?
3 What words and expressions does the writer use to ask for contributions?

your heart strings

For a fortunate few, *Symphony* provides comfortable retirement homes for musicians no longer able to look after themselves. With like-minded people they can revisit their triumphs and live in dignity.

WE NEED YOUR HELP

Symphony homes are funded by people like you. To continue our work we rely on donations and money left to us in wills. We ask you to remember the musicians who have given so much pleasure. Once they received your applause – now they need your financial support.

To make a donation, phone 0732 81930 now. Aren't you happy that you decided to help?

sympathy isn't enough.

WRITING

5 Imagine that you work for an advertising agency. Someone wants to raise money for a charity for diabetes. This is the information they give you.

Millions of people suffer from diabetes. It can strike young children as well as older people. Some people have to have two painful injections of insulin each day to keep them alive. Mothers often have to do this to their babies who can't understand what is going on. Diabetics are more likely to suffer serious illness and early death than other groups. Please be as generous as you can to help us find a way of curing this terrible disease.

Work in pairs or groups. Improve the text by making it more personal and getting the reader to identify with the sufferer.

6 Imagine that you wanted to make the text into a poster. What image(s) would you choose?

SPEAKING

7 You are going to plan a campaign for a charity of your choice. Organise yourselves into groups according to the charity you wish to support. If you like, you can choose one from this list.
the homeless   the blind   the third world
protection of the environment   animal rights

8 Now discuss the following.
1 Often famous people agree to be the public face of charities. Choose a famous person to be your sponsor or patron. How would you ask them to be your patron? What reasons would you give for choosing them?
2 What sort of events would be a good way of getting publicity or raising money for your campaign? Possibilities: a parade, concerts, sponsored runs, parachute jumps. Think of some others.
3 How could you win the support of people from different ages, groups and backgrounds?

WRITING

9 You want to run an advertising campaign in newspapers and magazines on behalf of your charity. In your groups, plan the following.
1 The 'copy' (what you say) which should be no more than 100 words.
2 Decide which members of the public you want to reach and what you want to say.
3 Choose the papers and magazines in which to put your advertisement.
4 Make your 'copy' as involving and as personal as you can.
5 Decide which images you would use to accompany the advertisement.
6 Think carefully about layout and the use of colour.

Write the advertisement and design the poster.

Grammar reference

1 The infinitive

We use the infinitive with *to*:

- after some common verbs: *afford, agree, dare, decide, hope, intend, manage, need, pretend, promise, offer, seem, refuse, tend, threaten, want, wish, would like.*
  EXAMPLE: *We **managed to repair** the car.*

- after the modal verbs *ought* and *have (got)*.
  EXAMPLE: *You **ought to listen** to what she says.*

- in clauses of purpose.
  EXAMPLES: *She went to the shop **to buy** some bread. He took off his shoes so as **not to wake** the baby.*

- with some verbs followed by an object: *advise, allow, ask, command, encourage, expect, force, help, invite, order, permit, persuade, remind, teach, tell, want, warn.*
  EXAMPLES: *They encouraged him **to play** the piano. She told the boy not **to leave** the door open.*

The infinitive without *to* is used:

- after the modal verbs *can, could, may, might, must, shall, should, will, would, needn't* (But *need **to***).
  EXAMPLES: ***Can** you **hear** me? I **might** not go to the party.*

- after the verbs *make* and *let*.
  EXAMPLES: *His mother **made** him **do** the washing-up. She **let** him **watch** TV.*
  Notice that in the passive we say:
  *He **was made to do** the washing-up. He **was allowed to watch** TV. (Let does not exist in the passive.)*

- after the expression *had better*.
  EXAMPLE: *We **had better go**, it's getting late.*

2 The -ing form

The -ing form is used:

- after most verbs of liking and disliking: *enjoy, like, love, dislike, detest, dread, hate, mind, can't stand.*
  EXAMPLES: *I really **enjoy singing** in the choir. Would you **mind answering** a few questions?*

- after some other common verbs: *admit, avoid, come, consider, deny, finish, go, involve, miss, postpone, risk, suggest.*
  EXAMPLES: *He **denied stealing** the money. Let's **go swimming**.*

- after prepositions, including adjective + preposition phrases, e.g. *fed up with, keen on, tired of.*
  EXAMPLES: *Don't cross the road **without looking**! This knife should only be used **for cutting** meat. I'm **tired of listening** to her complaints.*

- after phrasal verbs.
  EXAMPLE: *I've **given up learning** Japanese.*

- after verb patterns ending in a preposition, e.g. *accuse someone of, congratulate someone on.*
  EXAMPLE: *She **accused me of lying**.*

3 Phrasal verbs

- A phrasal verb consists of a verb plus one or two particles. (A particle is either a preposition or an adverb.)
  EXAMPLES: *to look after someone* (= to take care of) *to give up* (= to stop)

We can divide phrasal verbs into four types, according to how they behave grammatically.

- Type 1 phrasal verbs are intransitive – they cannot take a direct object.
  EXAMPLES: *Their money **ran out**.* (= was all used up) *In spite of the rain, the parade **went ahead**.*

The other three types of phrasal verbs are all transitive – they can have a direct object.

- Type 2 phrasal verbs consist of a verb plus a particle, e.g. *switch off, pick up, knock down*. They are separable, which means that a noun or pronoun object can come between the two parts of the verb. If the direct object is a noun, it has two possible positions, either between the two parts of the verb or at the end.
  EXAMPLES: *He **switched** the lights **off**. He **switched off** the lights.*
  But if the direct object is a pronoun, it MUST come between the two parts of the verb.
  EXAMPLE: *He **switched** them **off**.* (NOT **He switched off them.*)

- Type 3 phrasal verbs consist of a verb plus a particle, e.g. *look for, look after, get over*. They are inseparable, which means that the direct object MUST come at the end of the phrasal verb.
  EXAMPLES: *She's **getting over** the illness.* (NOT **She's getting the illness over.*)
  *She's **getting over** it.* (NOT **She's getting it over.*)
  The main difficulty is deciding whether they are Type 2 or Type 3.

- Type 4 phrasal verbs have two particles, an adverb and a preposition, e.g. *get round to, put up with, look forward to*. However, they are easy to use because they are always inseparable, like Type 3 verbs.
  EXAMPLES: *They are **looking forward to** a long holiday. They are **looking forward to** it.*

Progress check Units 10–11

GRAMMAR AND FUNCTIONS

1 Write first or zero conditional sentences by expanding the prompts.

1 Unless you/move/the car you/get/a parking ticket.
2 Meat/soon go/bad if you/leave/it in a warm place.
3 That meat/go/bad if you/leave/it there.
4 If I/see/him I/give/him your message.
5 When the adverts/come on/I/usually make/ a cup of coffee.

2 Andy and Rachel are on holiday in London. Fill each gap in their conversation with one word.

ANDY: What ¹..... we do today? ²..... you like to take a boat trip on ³..... Thames?
RACHEL: Not really. I'd ⁴..... visit a museum.
ANDY: OK. How about ⁵..... Natural History Museum, where the dinosaurs ⁶..... ?
RACHEL: Well, if you don't ⁷..... , I'd ⁸..... to go to the Victoria and Albert Museum to see the costume collection.
ANDY: That's fine by me. ⁹..... we go by tube?
RACHEL: No, ¹⁰.....'s go by bus. I prefer ¹¹..... able to see where I'm going, don't ¹²..... ?

3 Complete the phrasal verbs by adding either the verb or the particle.

1 Don't worry, you'll soon ..... over your cold.
2 Could you pick my glasses ..... ? They're by your feet.
3 'Do you think Matthew will ..... up late again?' 'Well, he's almost always late, so it's likely!'
4 Can you look ..... my wallet and keys while I go swimming?
5 I really can't ..... up with his behaviour any more; it's awful!
6 We loaded the car, looked at the map and ..... off.

Now rewrite the sentences, replacing the noun object with a pronoun, if possible.

1 Don't worry, you'll soon get over it.

4 Put the adjectives in brackets in the correct position in the sentences.

1 I'm looking forward to a hot shower. (nice)
2 She was wearing a short silk jacket. (greenish)
3 The round piece of gold turned out to be a(n) Greek coin. (tiny/ancient)
4 What a pretty girl! (little)
5 I'd love a glass of white wine. (ice-cold)

5 Complete these sentences with the correct form of the verb in brackets.

1 Did you persuade your sister (hold) the party in her house?
2 Jack's father made him (eat) his vegetables.
3 She denied (break) the lawn mower.
4 We must (fix) that window. It's dangerous the way it is.
5 Will you please stop (make) that terrible noise. I'm trying (work).
6 His teacher encouraged him (apply) for university.
7 Oh dear! She seems (be) out – nobody is answering the phone.
8 Are you accusing me of (tell) lies?
9 Hurry up! We can't risk (miss) the train.
10 She avoided (catch) a cold last winter by taking lots of vitamin C.
11 It's a waste of time (knock). They've all gone out.
12 We'd better (go) home. I think I forgot (turn off) the cooker.

VOCABULARY

6 Choose the correct alternative in *italics* to complete each sentence.

1 Guests are reminded that *precious/valuable* personal belongings should not be left in their rooms.
2 We are proud of the *human/humane* treatment of our prisoners.
3 She was wearing a *blue as sky/sky-blue* blouse.
4 All his advice turned out to be *worthless/ priceless.*
5 No one could resist his *boyish/childish* good looks.

New cultures

Watch your manners!

GETTING STARTED

1 In which cultures do people:

1 have an afternoon siesta?
2 drink lots of tea?
3 play boules?
4 eat outside?
5 start work at 6.00 a.m?

2 What habits do foreigners consider to be characteristic of your culture?

LISTENING

3 📼 Marcello is talking to Julia about how to behave in England. Make notes about the following.

1 driving
2 queuing
3 saying *please* and *thank you*
4 what to call people
5 greeting people

4 📼 Listen again, and make notes of all the questions that Julia asks Marcello. You will need your notes for Exercise 8.

DISCOVERING LANGUAGE

5 Match these three sentences using *used to* with the descriptions, a)–c).

1 He used to live in London.
2 He's used to living in London.
3 He got used to living in London.

a) At first life wasn't easy, but then he learned how to live in London.
b) He lived in London for a while, but doesn't any more.
c) He doesn't find life in London strange now.

6 Marisa is an au pair in an English family in London. In return for food and accommodation she looks after the children, drives them to school and does some housework. Make sentences, using one or more of the three forms of *used to*, based on what she says.

1 When I lived in my country I got up at eight o'clock; now I have to get up at six-thirty.
2 At first driving on the left was difficult, but now I think it's OK.
3 The weather here is terrible. Even if I lived here for fifty years, I would still miss the sunshine of back home.
4 The English queue for everything. At first it was strange, but now if I see a queue, I automatically join it.
5 English food is very different from the food of my own country, but now I am starting to enjoy it!
6 I cried for my parents every night for three weeks, but now I feel OK about being away.

⟳ COMPARING CULTURES

7 Work in groups. Discuss what someone from a completely different culture would have to get used to if they came to live in your country. Think about:

the weather   food   driving   security
working hours   sleeping times   queuing
greeting people

Now make a list and put the things in order of difficulty: the easiest first, the most difficult last.

SPEAKING

8 Work in pairs.
Student A: You are speaking to a foreigner about how they find living in your country. Ask questions about the topics in Exercise 3. Adapt some of the questions Julia asked Marcello. Ask where they used to live; about the things they have got used to; the things they are still getting used to or will *never* get used to!
Student B: Imagine you are a foreigner who has lived in your present country for *two* years. Decide where you come from and how you used to live in your old country. Look at the notes you made in Exercise 3. Decide the things you have already got used to; are still getting used to and, perhaps, those you will *never* get used to! Answer your partner's questions.

FOCUS ON FUNCTIONS

9 In a foreign culture it is sometimes possible to appear rude completely by accident. Look at the questions and replies below.

The questions are asked by someone you don't know very well. There are two possible replies. Both replies are grammatically correct, but which one *could* offend an English person?

1 Does this bus go to town?
  a) I don't think so.   b) No, it doesn't.
2 Do you speak English?
  a) Yes, of course.   b) Yes, I do.
3 You're German, aren't you?
  a) Actually, I'm Swiss.
  b) No, I'm not. I'm Swiss.
4 Is it OK if I smoke?
  a) No, it isn't.   b) I'd rather you didn't.
5 Have you got a pen I could borrow?
  a) No, I haven't.   b) I'm afraid not.
6 How are you?
  a) Fine, thanks. How are you?   b) Awful.
7 Would you like a cigarette?
  a) No, thanks.   b) No, I wouldn't.
8 Would you like to come to the cinema tomorrow?
  a) Sorry, no. I'm very busy.
  b) I'm afraid I'm busy. What a pity.
9 Can I make a phone call?
  a) Yes, OK.   b) Yes, of course.

10 📼 Now listen to the polite responses on the cassette and find out if you were right.

SPEAKING

11 Work in pairs and practise being polite.
Student A: You are 'someone' in these situations. Make questions or sentences from the prompts.
Student B: Contradict your partner or say *no* gently using expressions from Exercise 9. Think carefully about using the right tone of voice and intonation.

1 Someone says that you are married. Tell them you are single.
2 Someone asks if they can open the window. Say *no* giving a reason.
3 Someone invites you for dinner. Refuse, giving a reason.
4 Someone says that the lesson starts at five. Tell them they are wrong.
5 Someone asks if you can do something you know you do well, e.g. play tennis; drive.
6 Someone asks after your health. You have got a slight headache!

Far from home

Focus

TOPIC
• Different cultures

GRAMMAR
• Future progressive

SKILLS
• Listening: a monologue
• Reading: data
• Speaking: making predictions

VOCABULARY DEVELOPMENT
• Words related to immigration

GETTING STARTED

1 Imagine that you are going to live abroad for a long time.

1 Which things and which people would you miss the most? Do you think you would get homesick?
2 What, if anything, would you take with you to remind you of home?
3 What would worry you most about leaving home?
4 Which typical objects from your country would you take as small gifts?

DEVELOPING VOCABULARY

2 Discuss these questions.

1 What is the difference between *immigration* and *emigration*?
2 What do we call the people who:
  a) immigrate?   b) emigrate?

3 Match the parts of these sentences.

1 If someone is hospitable,
2 If someone is a refugee,
3 When someone is prejudiced,
4 When someone suffers from discrimination,
5 If someone is racist,
6 If someone lives in exile,

a) they dislike you because of your race.
b) they live with injustice.
c) their government has forced them to leave their own country.
d) they welcome you into their homes.
e) they have had to leave their country because of war or famine.
f) they have unfair and unfavourable opinions which they haven't thought about deeply.

SPEAKING

4 Work in pairs. Discuss these questions.

1 How easy is it for foreigners to settle in your country?
2 How hospitable is your country to foreigners in general and refugees in particular?
3 Are any groups of people victims of prejudice and discrimination?
4 If you had to leave your own country, which country would you choose to live in?

🔲 Documentary

LISTENING

5 📼 Joan Tull from London is going to work for Voluntary Service Overseas (VSO) in Zimbabwe. VSO sends volunteers to work in other countries for two or three years.

1 Why does Joan want to do VSO?
2 Do you think she is a good choice of candidate?

6 📼 Joan describes what she'll be doing.

1 What will her duties be?
2 How long is her contract?

FACT-FILE

Zimbabwe

- **Population**
10 million. Mainly Bantu.
- **Capital city**
Harare.
- **Languages**
English (official language), Chishona, Sindebele.
- **Religions**
Muslim, Hindu, Animist, Christian.
- **Geography**
Zimbabwe is a land-locked country in south-east Africa, mostly on a high plateau. The Zambezi River in the north and the Limpopo River in the south form natural borders.

- **Climate**
Tropical. Dry season June to September.
- **History**
Once the site of the ancient kingdom of Zimbabwe. Colonised by British under Cecil Rhodes from 1890s. Regained independence in 1980.
- **Economy**
Mainly agricultural – tobacco, sugar cane, tea, wheat and maize.
Mining – gold, asbestos, nickel, coal.

READING

7 Now look at the fact-file about Zimbabwe.

1 What do you think would be easy or difficult in Zimbabwe for someone brought up in London?
2 How would someone from your own culture find it?

LISTENING

8 Look at the topics below. What do you think Joan will say about the differences between London and Zimbabwe?

1 technology
2 living in a city/in the country
3 choice of food
4 water and electricity
5 entertainment

⌨ **Now listen and check your answers.**

9 ⌨ Listen to the next part of the interview.

1 What does she think her biggest problem will be?
2 How do you think she will adapt?

SPEAKING

10 Work in pairs. Discuss these questions.

1 Would you ever consider doing VSO?
2 If you did, where would you like to go?
3 How would a future employer in your country view this sort of experience? Would they be enthusiastic or suspicious?

DISCOVERING LANGUAGE

11 Look at this sentence from the Documentary, which uses the future progressive.

I'll be teaching English in Zimbabwe.

1 Is Joan making a spontaneous decision or talking about something that has already been arranged or decided?
2 Is Joan confident in her prediction?
3 How is the future progressive tense formed?

12 Work in pairs and take turns to do the following.

Student A: Make predictions about someone in your class. *Don't* give the person's name! Predict the life they will be living at these different ages: 30, 50 and 70.

'When you're thirty you'll be married, you'll be living on a farm in the country.'

Student B: Try to guess who your partner is describing.

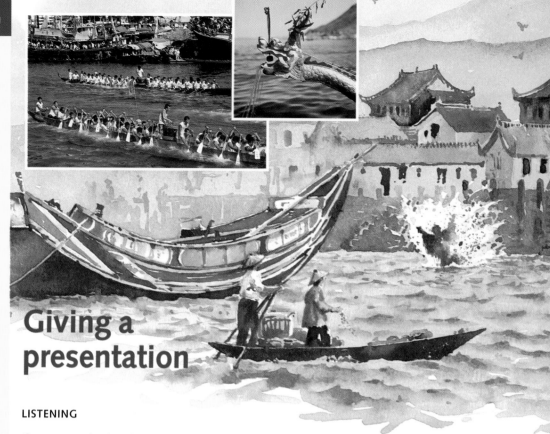

Focus

TOPIC
• Festivals

SKILLS
• Listening: a presentation
• Reading: a presentation
• Speaking: asking for and giving information/ giving a presentation

SPEECH PATTERNS
• Giving new information: intonation

Giving a presentation

LISTENING

1 Lucy Naylor has been invited back to her old school to tell the pupils about a trip she made to the Far East. She is going to talk about the festival in the pictures. Before you listen, discuss where the festival takes place and what it is about. What connection do you think there could be between the pictures?

2 📼 Now listen and make notes about the following.

1 The name of the event.
2 When and where it takes place.
3 Its origins.
4 The preparations.
5 The people involved.
6 The atmosphere.
7 What actually happens.
8 Lucy's general opinion of the event.

READING

3 Read Lucy's presentation and complete the text by using each of these words and expressions once only.

before   in fact   afterwards   actually
let me explain   you know   incidentally
anyway   returning   once upon a time
you can imagine   first of all   nowadays

❝Good evening, everybody. I am going to tell you something about my travels to the Far East. As ¹....., I saw a lot of festivals, but the one I'm going to tell you about is the Dragon Boat Festival, which takes place in the middle of the summer in Hong Kong; it's an absolutely marvellous setting for the event. There are other races throughout China, but this one attracts the most foreign spectators.

²....., ³..... I carry on, I should say a few words about dragons. They are very important symbols in Chinese myth and legend. ⁴..... people used to believe that rain was made by dragons fighting up in the skies! ⁵....., going back to the festival, it's also known as 'Poet's Day'. ⁶.... how it got this name: long ago there was a wise man and poet called Qu Yuan who threw himself into the Mi Lo river as a protest against corruption. People went out in boats to save him, but he drowned. Fishermen threw rice into the river so sharks wouldn't eat his body. ⁷..... his ghost came and told the fishermen that the best way to scare away bad spirits

was to wrap up little parcels of rice in silk.
[8]....., in memory of the poet, people eat special
rice dumplings wrapped up in leaves.

[9].... to the festival itself, the event that
attracts so many visitors is the dragon boat
race. Dragon boats are rowing boats with a
carved dragon's head on the front. Each boat
has two lines of rowers who paddle furiously
while someone beats time on an enormous
drum – [10]....., the race is taken very seriously.
It's an international event too; although most
teams come from the region, some are from as
far apart as France, South Africa and New
Zealand! [11].... there are so many that there
are lots of 'heats', [12].....– qualifying races –
before a team can get to the final.

When I went the men's final was won by an
Indonesian team, while a team from Canada
won the women's. It was an exciting climax to
the event. [13]....., I cheered and shouted so
much that I lost my voice!

If you'd like to gather round, I've got some
photos here which will give you a better idea of
what actually goes on. I've also brought some
rice dumplings in for everyone to try, so help
yourselves. Are there any questions? "

**4 Answer the questions to see how Lucy's
presentation is organised. How does Lucy:**

1 signal she is about to start her presentation?
2 state her purpose?
3 introduce less important pieces of information?
4 change topic?
5 refer to the old days and modern times?
6 return to the subject of her presentation?

**5 Read the second paragraph of the presentation
again and make questions for these answers.**

1 That rain was made by fighting dragons.
2 As a protest.
3 So sharks wouldn't eat his body.
4 By making parcels of rice.

SPEAKING

6 Work in pairs.
Student A: Make questions to ask B based on the
third paragraph of the presentation. Answer B's
questions.
Student B: Make questions to ask A based on the
final two paragraphs. Answer A's questions.

SPEECH PATTERNS

7 🔲 **Listen to Lucy's presentation again.**
What do you notice about Lucy's intonation at the
beginning of each new paragraph? Is it higher or
lower than at the end of the paragraph before it?

SPEAKING

**8 Imagine you are going to give a presentation
to a group of foreigners about a festival from
your country or region.**

1 Make notes under these headings.
   a) The name of the festival.
   b) The time of year it takes place.
   c) Its origins/history (if you know them).
   d) How people prepare for it:
      • clothes/costumes
      • food: any special dishes you eat at the
        festival
      • other attractions, e.g. a parade/fireworks
2 When your teacher has checked your notes
   think of how you are going to make the talk
   more interesting. Is there anything you can
   bring to class, e.g. pictures or costumes?

**9 Using Lucy's presentation as a guide, give a
presentation about your festival.**

Grammar reference

1 *Used to* as a verb

- *Used to* is a verb which only exists in the past simple form. We use it to describe past habits and regular actions which no longer happen.
  EXAMPLES: *He **used to smoke** thirty cigarettes a day.* (but now he doesn't)
  *When I was a child, we never **used to have holidays.***
- *Used to* can also describe past states.
  EXAMPLES: *She **used to be very thin** when she was younger.*
  *We **used to live** in a wonderful villa by the sea.*

FORM

- *Used to* is followed by an infinitive. It has the same form for all persons: *I used to, you used to, he used to,* etc.
- We form the interrogative and negative in the same way as regular verbs.
  EXAMPLES: *Did you **use to** live in Paris? Yes, I did.*
  *Where did you **use to** live?*
  *We didn't **use to** have holidays.* or, more common
  We never used to have holidays.
  *Didn't you **use to** live in a villa? Yes, we did.*

2 *Used to* as an adjective

- *Used to* is also an adjective phrase with the same meaning as *accustomed to* or *familiar with.*
  EXAMPLES: *I'm **used to** the British weather.*
  *I hated my job at first, but I'm **used to** it now.*
  *Are you **used to** waiting in queues?*
- *Get used to* is commonly used to express the process of becoming accustomed to something.
  EXAMPLE: *It took her several years to **get used to** the hot weather.*

FORM

- *Used* as an adjective takes the preposition *to* followed by a noun, pronoun or the *-ing* form. It usually follows the verbs *be, become* or *get*:
  to be + used + to + noun/pronoun/ -ing form
  Because *to* is a preposition here, it CANNOT be followed by the infinitive form of a verb, only the *-ing* form:
  EXAMPLE: *You'll soon get used to driving on the left.*
  (NOT ** to drive on the left.*)

3 The future progressive

- We use the future progressive to predict a continuous action or situation that will be in progress at a particular time in the future.
  EXAMPLES: *This time next week I'**ll be lying** on a beach in Corfu.*
  *Next time you see me I **won't be wearing** glasses.*

FORM

- The form of the future progressive is:
  will + *be* + present participle (*-ing* form)
  Notice these questions and negative forms:
  *What **will** you **be wearing**?*
  ***Will** you **be wearing** trousers?*
  ***Won't** you **be wearing** a skirt?*
  *I **won't be wearing** jeans.*
- We can also use adverbs such as *probably* and *definitely* with the future progressive to express different degrees of certainty about our predictions.
  EXAMPLES: *He'**ll probably be driving** his new car.*
  *I **definitely won't be living** in this flat next year.*
  Notice the position of the adverb – between *will* and *be* in a positive sentence, but before *won't* in a negative sentence.
- We can also use expressions like *I hope, I expect* and *I think* before the future progressive when we are not completely certain.
  EXAMPLE: *I **think** he'**ll be waiting** for me.* (but I'm not sure)
- The future progressive is often used to show that something will be in progress if or when something else happens in the future.
  EXAMPLES: *If you need me, I'**ll be waiting** by the telephone.*
  *When you see me again, I'**ll be living** in my new flat.*

Talkback

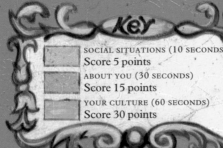

Functioning well!

1 Work in groups of four. Student A asks the questions and Students B, C and D answer them.

Student A: Find a watch with a second hand. YOU choose two questions for each player from each category. Each question can only be used once. Make sure players keep to the time limits.

Students B, C and D: Answer the questions. You score points *only* if you answer in the time limit.

1 You find a magic lamp and the genie gives you three wishes; quickly say what they would be.

2 Give a strong opinion about something e.g. dogs in cities, smoking in restaurants.

3 Talk about a festival in your town or country.

4 Describe the qualities of an ideal partner!

5 Somebody says that they agree with capital punishment. Agree or disagree strongly.

6 Talk about your plans or ambitions for the future.

7 Speak about your most precious possession.

8 Your friend didn't turn up for an appointment and didn't even phone you. Criticise him/her!

9 Somebody wants to borrow your camera or CD player. Agree but make two strong conditions.

10 Congratulate someone on a piece of good news.

11 Talk about a really frightening experience.

12 Give a traditional recipe from your country.

13 Tell everybody what your duties are at school or at work.

14 Talk about a national or sporting hero.

15 You're on a train and someone asks if they can open the window. Say 'no' politely, giving a reason.

16 An elderly person is finding it difficult to carry some shopping. Offer to help.

17 Somebody says a painting is by Picasso. Tell them gently that they're wrong.

18 Tell everybody about an embarrassing experience.

19 Refuse an invitation to dinner politely, giving a good excuse.

20 Talk about a time when somebody forced you to do something against your will.

21 You're in a TV room in a hotel. Ask permission from the other people to turn onto another channel.

22 Express two regrets about things you did in the past which were a big mistake.

23 Give the rules of a game which is special to your country, e.g. cricket in England, Pelota in Spain.

24 Describe somebody you admire and say why.

25 Talk about three childhood habits.

26 Your friend has just failed his/her driving test for the second time. Be sympathetic.

27 Talk about a dream or nightmare.

28 A tourist asks you if you speak English. Reply modestly that you do!

29 Somebody offers to take you to the theatre or a football match. State your preference.

30 Describe your favourite painting or photograph.

31 A foreign visitor asks you the best way of spending two weeks in your country. Give some advice.

32 Say what you'd do if you were president for a day.

33 Give a foreign visitor advice about table manners and how to greet people in your country.

34 You're in the library; somebody is writing in a reference book. Politely tell them not to.

35 Explain how a simple machine, which you own, works.

36 Summarise your favourite book or film.

Gone missing?

GETTING STARTED

1 Look at the pictures of three famous places. Can you identify them?

1 Which are real? Which are legendary?
2 What were they famous for?
3 What mysteries are associated with them?

2 🔊 Now listen and find out if you were right.

🔄 COMPARING CULTURES

3 Work in pairs. Discuss these questions.

1 What famous/mysterious places are there in your country?
2 Are there any myths or legends which surround them?

DEVELOPING VOCABULARY

4 Choose the correct words for these sentences. In one sentence both answers are correct. Which one is it?

1 When they were in the attic they *found out/came across* some old paintings.
2 One theory is that Atlantis was *lost/vanished* in a volcanic eruption. One minute it was there, the next it had *vanished/lost*.
3 The explorers *discovered/found out* the lost city in the middle of a sea of sand dunes.
4 They *found out/discovered* the identity of the knight from a manuscript.

📺 **Documentary**

5 Look at the pictures and discuss them with your partner. Use some of these words and expressions.

It could be   It might be   It can't be
It looks like   Perhaps   I'm not sure, but
It looks as if   It must be

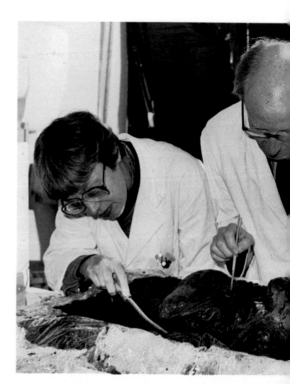

6 Read the text and glossary to find out more.

❝In the north of England, in a place called Lindow Moss, the body of a man was found. Because he had been buried in a peat bog his body was very well preserved. 'Lindow Man', as the body is called, is about two thousand years old.❞

GLOSSARY
peat: a kind of earth which has very good qualities of preservation. It is used in agriculture to enrich the soil. In some places peat is also burned as a fuel.
bog: an area of soft wet ground made from decaying vegetable matter.

LISTENING

7 📼 Listen to the archaeologist Rick Turner talking about the discovery of Lindow Man. Do the statements below refer to something *certain* (C), something *possible* (P), or something *impossible* (I)?

1 (The archaeologist thought at first that) the peat contained a whole body.
2 He had died of hunger.
3 He was killed by other people.
4 He was killed by being hit on the head.
5 He worked in the fields.
6 He was a bard (poet).

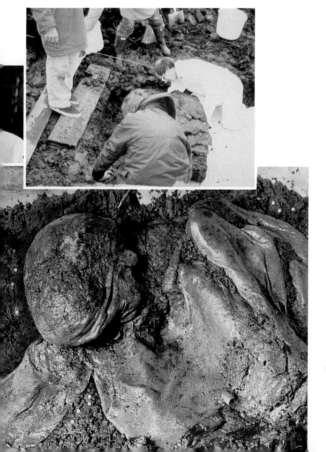

8 📼 Listen again and answer these questions.

1 How was Lindow Man discovered?
2 What were the archaeologists able to find out about him early on?
3 Which three injuries killed him?
4 What do the archaeologists know about him now the scientific tests have been completed?
5 How similar was he to people of today?
6 Why did he come to be in the bog?

DISCOVERING LANGUAGE

9 📼 Complete these two sentences about Lindow Man from the Documentary, then listen and check your answers.

    A *He ..... a bard.*
    B *He ..... someone who didn't work in the fields.*

1 Which words in the two sentences are:
    a) stressed?   b) contracted?

Now look at these two sentences.

    C *It could have been a ritualistic killing.*
    D *He can't have been very old.*

2 Which of the sentences, A–D, refers to:
    a) something possible?
    b) something almost certain?
    c) something impossible?

10 Look at your answers to Exercise 7 and rephrase the sentences to use the structures above.

1 *The peat might have contained a whole body.*

SPEAKING

11 Imagine that you are archaeologists and you find these objects in a cave. What do they tell us about the society in which they were used?

Is there anybody there?

Focus

TOPIC
• Mediums

GRAMMAR
• Defining and non-defining relative clauses

SKILLS
• Reading: a magazine article
• Listening: a conversation
• Speaking: giving an explanation

SPEECH PATTERNS
• Defining and non-defining relative clauses: intonation

GETTING STARTED

1 Work in pairs. Discuss these questions.

1 What happens to human spirits when we die?
2 Do you believe in the possible existence of ghosts and the supernatural?
3 Do you think it is possible to communicate with spirits? If you wanted to, how would you try to do so?

READING

2 Read the article and find out about Coral Polge's special gift. Can you think of any logical explanation for it?

3 Are these statements true or false?

1 Coral doesn't help people very much.
2 Although her portraits weren't good, she knew she'd become an artist.
3 Portraits of spirit guides proved she had psychic gifts.
4 Coral consciously decides what to draw.
5 Mrs Timms was immediately convinced of Coral's powers to contact the dead.

The remarkable CORAL POLGE

CORAL POLGE is a person *who* has provided comfort to thousands. She has a remarkable talent *which* may prove the survival of the human spirit after death. For Coral is a medium who draws the portraits of spirits who contact her.

Coral, *whose* parents were spiritualists, was brought up in Harrow, North London, where she attended a local spiritualist church. She studied art at the local college, *where* she specialised in textile design. Even though, at the time, she wasn't very good at drawing portraits, she met a medium who told her she would be a psychic artist.

She doesn't actually see the dead nor are her hands controlled by the spirits; instead she 'feels' them coming through. Early in her career she drew the portraits of 'spirit guides' from *whom* she had received help. These portraits of guides, who included Red Indians, nuns and monks, were remarkable, yet could have been attributed to the working of a strong imagination. She also drew portraits by holding on to letters *that* had been written by people who had since died.

Coral says, 'I know exactly what to draw without thinking about it. It's involuntary, like breathing or walking.' Not only are her portraits a good likeness but she sketches her subjects in clothes they would have worn in life.

Coral has displayed her talent at public meetings around the world. At one gathering there was a woman whose grandfather had just died. Her name was Phyllis Timms. Coral made a sketch of a man who had a long moustache and Phyllis recognised the man as her grandfather. However, she was reluctant to acknowledge the portrait without extra proof. Coral then said that the colour green was a link with the man whom she had drawn. Mrs Timms, whose maiden name had been Green, understood the significance of the comment and claimed the portrait.

There are some people for whom this is evidence of survival from beyond the grave. Others, who have their reservations, may put it down to an extraordinary kind of extrasensory perception. Whatever the reason, it remains a gift impossible to explain away and we should try to keep an open mind.

REVIEWING LANGUAGE

4 Look at these sentences from the article.

*Coral Polge is a person **who** has provided comfort to thousands. She has a remarkable talent **which** may prove the survival of the human spirit after death.*

1 Do the relative pronouns in **bold italics** refer to people or to things?
2 Find six different relative pronouns in the article.
   a) What do the pronouns in *italics* refer to?
   b) Which ones are for people, things, places and possession?
3 Look at this sentence where there is no relative pronoun.
   She sketches her subjects in clothes they'd have worn in life.
   a) Where could you put a relative pronoun if you wanted to?
   b) Which pronoun could you use?
   c) Why has it been omitted?

5 Join these pairs of sentences using an appropriate relative pronoun.

1 She studied art at the local college. She specialised in textile design.
2 She met a medium. He told her she would be a psychic artist.
3 She drew portraits of 'spirit guides'. She had received their help.
4 She drew portraits by holding on to letters. The letters had been written by people who had since died.
5 At one gathering there was a woman. Her grandfather had just died.
6 Coral made a sketch of a man. He had a long moustache.
7 The colour green was a link with the man. Coral had drawn him.

Now check your sentences with the article. What happens to *who* if it comes after a preposition?

DISCOVERING LANGUAGE

6 Look at this pair of sentences.

A *The medium, who was Italian, was very impressive.*
B *The medium who was Italian was very impressive.*

1 In which sentence:
   a) are there several mediums and only one was impressive?
   b) is there only one medium?
2 In which sentence:
   a) could we remove the relative clause without affecting its meaning?
   b) do we have to keep the relative clause?
3 Which sentence:
   a) has essential information (i.e. a defining relative clause)?
   b) has non-essential information (i.e. a non-defining relative clause)?

7 Find other examples of non-defining relative clauses in the article.

SPEECH PATTERNS

8 Listen to the sentences from Exercise 6.

1 Which sentence is said first, A or B?
2 Where do the pauses come?
3 Where does the voice fall in each sentence?

9 Combine these pairs of sentences by using a defining or non-defining relative clause.

1 We stayed in a famous haunted house last year. It was in the middle of nowhere.
2 I know a man. The man believes he can contact spirits.
3 That's the woman. Her parents are spiritualists.
4 The article about Coral Polge was from a very interesting book. I told you about it yesterday.

Now listen to the cassette and check your answers.

LISTENING

10 Listen to Antonio's story of a 'séance'. Are these statements true or false?

1 The people on the dig stayed in a hostel.
2 There wasn't much to do in the evenings.
3 They used some special equipment.
4 The spirit was called 'Charlene'.
5 Kurt appeared frightened.
6 The spirit spelt out Kurt's name.
7 It was easy to find Kurt.
8 Kurt was calm and composed.
9 They later found out all about the girl.

SPEAKING

11 Think of an explanation for what happened during and after the séance.

Writing an essay (1)

Focus

TOPIC
- The past

FUNCTIONS
- Defining terms
- Stating organisation
- Ordering arguments
- Giving examples
- Drawing conclusions
- Stating contrast

SKILLS
- Speaking: selecting arguments
- Reading: an essay
- Writing: a first draft of an essay

GETTING STARTED

1 Look at this essay title. Discuss exactly what it means.

'We are obsessed by the past.' Discuss this statement (maximum 400 words).

Study the ideas below that the writer 'brainstormed' (quickly noted). Work in pairs and decide which ones would be most suitable to:

a) agree with/support the statement.

b) disagree with the statement.

Be prepared to justify your choices.

1 In Britain, people prefer old houses, furniture, cars, etc.

2 Cost of archaeological digs worthwhile. Good to know about past.

3 Many people afraid of future – live in the past.

4 The desire for change is natural to human beings.

5 Human beings naturally optimistic.

6 Only snobs believe the old is better than new.

7 People are happy to invest in the future. Keep having children.

8 Childhood memories – far too important.

Add more ideas to the list.

2 Imagine you are going to write an essay using the ideas in Exercise 1. Which arguments do you think are important (I), of secondary importance (S) and unimportant (U)?

READING

3 Quickly read the essay and notice which ideas on the original list the writer didn't use. Are there any extra ideas which don't appear on the list?

First, we should define our terms of reference. Let us begin by taking the meaning of the word 'obsessed'. To be obsessed with something indicates an unhealthy, unreasonable interest. The 'we' of the question I am taking to mean my own culture. I shall first examine the evidence which supports the statement and then go on to consider arguments which counter it.

Without doubt people value the past. To begin with, let us consider the commercial value attached to all that is old. For instance, antique furniture and veteran cars fetch stunningly high prices at auctions. Old properties in good condition frequently command far higher prices than their contemporary equivalents. In addition, this preference for the past over the present, the old over the new, extends to the world of ideas. A classical education is still regarded by many as the peak of academic achievement.

Despite all this, we may not be quite as in love with the past as some people think. Quite simply, human nature survives on hope. After all, it could be argued that every child that is born is a vote of confidence in the future. Moreover, hope undoubtedly concerns the future, not the past. This is borne out by the fact that far more effort and money are invested in the future than are spent on the past. Just consider, for example, the tremendous advances which have been made in medicine and science. In addition, human beings have a natural curiosity and desire for experimentation and change. They cannot stand still for long. On a day-to-day level just consider the vitality of fashion, and pop music. They demonstrate that people are unwilling to stay rooted in the past.

In conclusion, we see that the past does have an influence on our lives and is generally valued. However; on balance, more people are concerned with the present and the future. If we were truly obsessed with the past, society would simply not progress. Therefore the statement must be wrong.

(334 words)

FOCUS ON FUNCTIONS

4 Read the essay again. How does the writer:
a) define his terms (*Paragraph 1*)?
b) state how the essay will be organised
   (*Paragraph 1*)?
c) put arguments in order?
d) add extra ideas?
e) give examples?
f) draw a logical conclusion to an argument?
g) say *but*?

FOCUS ON STYLE

5 The essay follows a traditional model. Look at the plan the writer followed. Which sentences in the essay correspond to the notes below?

PARAGRAPH 1

Definition of terms and statement of objectives

Introduction – define terms: *obsession* = something unhealthy; *we* = my culture

PARAGRAPH 2

Arguments in favour

Old things/ideas valued. *Examples* – things: antiques, etc.; ideas: classical education

PARAGRAPH 3

Arguments against

People survive on hope related to future; societies move on – interested in scientific advances: pop music/fashion

PARAGRAPH 4

Conclusion

Influenced by past, but more evidence suggests NOT obsessed by the past

6 Study the way Paragraph 2 is organised.

PARAGRAPH 2:
a) begins with a general statement:
   Without doubt people value the past.
b) supports the general statement with examples:
   commercial value of old furniture, cars and property
c) moves to a secondary theme:
   ideas and education

Now look at Paragraph 3 and identify the general statement, supporting argument and secondary theme in the same way.

7 Look at another essay title.
'Far too much money is spent on preserving old buildings and historic sites.' Discuss.

Work in pairs. Which of the ideas below:
a) support the statement?
b) are against the statement?
c) are important?
d) are of secondary importance?
e) *wouldn't* you use?

  1 Complete waste of money.
  2 Could use the money to build schools and
    hospitals.
  3 Tourism good for the economy.
  4 Makes children proud of the past.
  5 Helps to give us a cultural identity.
  6 What is an old building?
  7 Need to understand the past to understand
    ourselves.
  8 Makes people nationalistic.
  9 Children should play and not study the past.
10 Worry too much about preserving the past.

Add more ideas to the list if you can.

WRITING

8 Look back at the exercises on these two pages. What stages of planning an essay are illustrated? For example, the first stage might be analysing the title. Now plan your own four-paragraph essay based on the title in Exercise 7.

9 Now write the first draft of your essay. Remember to:

a) define your terms.
b) make general statements supported by specific examples.
c) use the words and expressions you analysed in Exercises 4, 5 and 6.

Grammar reference

1 *Must, can't, might* and *could*

- We use *must* (+ infinitive) when we conclude that something is true because it is logical, and *can't* (+ infinitive) when we conclude that something is untrue because it is impossible.
  EXAMPLES: *She looks just like him. She **must be** his sister.*
  *She **can't be** his sister. He's an only child.*
  *You **must be** very proud of your son.*
  Notice that the opposite of *must* here is *can't* (NOT *mustn't*).

- When we think something is possible we use the verbs *may*, *might* or *could* instead of *must*.
  EXAMPLE: *Where's Julie? She **could be** in the garden. Or she **might be** washing her hair.*

FORM

- The structure with *may*, *might* and *could* is the same as with *must* and *can't* (see above).

- To express negative speculation, we use *may not* or *might not* (but NOT *could not*).
  EXAMPLE: *That smoke alarm **may not be working**. You should have it checked.*

2 *Must/can't have* and *might/could have*

- We use *must have* (+ past participle) to say that we are almost certain about something in the past. We use *can't have* (+ past participle) when we think something in the past is impossible.
  EXAMPLES: *Melanie **must have taken** my keys by mistake.*
  *Peter **can't have been** serious when he said that.*

FORM

- The structure with *must have* and *can't have* is:
  must/can't + *have* + *been* + adjective
  been + *-ing* form
  other past participle, e.g.
  wanted, known.

- When we are speculating about the past but are less certain, we use *may have*, *might have* or *could have* instead of *must have*. We are saying that something was possible.
  EXAMPLES: *Are you sure Melanie took them? You **could have** left them at home.*
  *Peter **might have** been joking.*

- To express negative speculations about the past, we use *may not have* or *might not have* (but NOT *could not have*).
  EXAMPLE: *She **may not have** understood what you said. You should tell her again.*

3 Defining relative clauses

- We use relative clauses to join two ideas together into one sentence. They tell us more about the subject or object.
  EXAMPLES: *The man who lives next door is a writer. I've never met the man who lives next door.*

- A defining relative clause gives information which is essential to the meaning of the sentence. It defines or identifies who or what we are talking about.
  EXAMPLE: *She thanked the man who had helped her.*

FORM

- Defining relative clauses can begin with the following pronouns:
  who/that for people; *which/that* for things
  whose for possession (do not confuse with *who's*)
  where for place; *when* for time; *why* for reason
  EXAMPLES: *Is he the boy **who/that** you like?*
  *I'd like a suitcase **that** doesn't weigh very much.*
  *A widow is a woman **whose** husband has died.*
  *That's the restaurant **where** we ate yesterday.*
  *Do you remember the time **when** Jamie pushed you into the river?*
  *That was the reason **why** she couldn't come.*

- In defining relative clauses, the pronouns *who, which* and *that* can be omitted when they are the object of the verb in the relative clause.
  EXAMPLE: *Would you like to hear the CD (**which/that**) I bought today?*

- In written and formal English, *whom* can be used instead of *who* as an object pronoun.
  EXAMPLE: *Is he the boy **whom** you were telling me about?*

4 Non-defining relative clauses

- Non-defining relative clauses provide extra information which is not essential to the main meaning of the sentence. They are used mostly in written English, and are separated from the main clause by commas. (If they are spoken, the speaker pauses before and after the relative clause.)
  EXAMPLES: *John, who had never been abroad before, booked a safari holiday in Zimbabwe.*
  The Great Pyramid, which was built more than four thousand years ago, is one of the world's most mysterious buildings.

- The pronoun *that* cannot be used in non-defining relative clauses, and the relative pronoun cannot be omitted.

- A non-defining relative clause can come at the end of a sentence as well as in the middle. It is still separated from the main clause by a comma.
  EXAMPLE: *Near the pyramids is the famous Sphinx, which may represent one of the pharaohs.*

Progress check Units 12–13

1 Tarzan has come to England after living in the jungle for many years. Complete the sentences with *used to* and an appropriate form of the verb in brackets.

1 Tarzan . . . . . (have) bananas for breakfast, but now he has boiled eggs and toast.
2 When he arrived, he . . . . . (wear) clothes and they felt strange and uncomfortable.
3 In the jungle he . . . . . (swing) everywhere on a vine, but nowadays he . . . . . (travel) by car.
4 He didn't . . . . . (go) to parties, but now he has a wonderful social life.
5 He still . . . . . (not be) the weather in England; he thinks it is too cold.
6 At first, people . . . . . (stop) him in the street to ask him questions, but now they've . . . . . (see) him.

2 Complete the dialogue by expanding the prompts. Add articles, prepositions, etc. and put the verbs in the correct tense.

DEBBIE: What you/think/you do/five years' time?
ALAN: Well, I definitely/not work/car park attendant. I want/become/opera singer. I hope/I live/Milan/and sing/*La Scala*. What about you?
DEBBIE: Unless I pass/exams/I probably still serve/rude customers/Harrods.
ALAN: You/not be/very optimistic/be you?

3 Give negative but polite replies to these questions.

1 Would you like another piece of apple pie?
2 If you're not doing anything on Saturday, how about going to see the Picasso exhibition?
3 Would you mind if I turned the heating down?
4 Do you think you could lend me five dollars?
5 Have you got a map I could borrow?

4 Make complete sentences by matching the following parts.

1 An orphan is someone	a) where you are standing.
2 I'll have some of the cake	b) which comes from rainforests.
3 Obsidian is a hard black stone	c) who lives in a place.
4 We avoid using wood	d) whose parents have died.
5 An inhabitant is a person	e) Eileen made.
6 X marks the spot	f) that the Aztecs used for making knives.

5 Write sentences with *must, can't, may, might* or *could* for these situations.

I can't believe that you didn't see the red light!
You must have seen the red light.

1 James phones Amanda every day and often sends her flowers. I'm sure he's in love with her.
2 I'm almost certain that she didn't intend to be rude.
3 It's possible that they've gone away for the weekend.
4 Maybe you didn't understand.
5 Perhaps she was feeling ill.
6 It's five o'clock already! I can't believe it.
7 Where's John? He's never late unless he's been held up by the traffic.

6 Join each pair of sentences. Add commas if necessary. Omit the relative pronoun if you can.

My husband speaks fluent French and German. He comes from Switzerland.
My husband, who speaks fluent French and German, comes from Switzerland.

1 This is a picture of the man. He was seen running away from the scene of the crime.
2 We visited the Tower of London. It was built in the eleventh century.
3 Here is the book on birdwatching. You said you wanted to borrow it.
4 Many people left flowers outside the building. The woman had been killed there.
5 They're the couple. Their children caused all the damage.

14 *Future perfect?*

Science fiction or fact?

Focus

TOPIC
• The year 2025

GRAMMAR
• Future perfect

SKILLS
• Listening: a monologue
• Reading: future scenarios
• Writing: making notes/future scenario

A

B

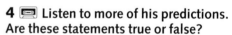

GETTING STARTED

1 Describe the different futures which these pictures suggest.

2 If you could turn back the clock, which three inventions or discoveries would you 'un-invent' and why?

🖭 Documentary

LISTENING

3 📼 Bruce Sterling is a science-fiction writer. Listen to him making predictions about the world in 2025. What is he interested in? Do you think he is an optimist or a pessimist?

Listen again and correct or modify these statements where necessary.

1 Europe will be the source of another world war.
2 There will be a single European currency.
3 The US and East Asia will still dominate the world.

4 📼 Listen to more of his predictions. Are these statements true or false?

1 We will still be polluting the environment.
2 Our diets will be similar to the one we have today.
3 We will not be killing animals for food.

5 📼 Listen to how he summarises the progress the human race will have made and complete the text.

❝ We will have become more ¹..... , but we will not have become any more ²..... . I think we will still see the same ³..... , the same ⁴..... , the same basic animal traits that have always ⁵..... humanity. But, on the other hand, I don't believe we will have become any ⁶..... and perhaps our increasing knowledge may bring us a little bit more ⁷..... . ❞

DISCOVERING LANGUAGE

6 Look at this sentence from the Documentary.
We will have become more advanced.
will have + infinitive (without *to*)

1 Are we advanced at the moment? What does Bruce hope will happen?
2 Will we be more advanced in 2025?
3 Is an exact date mentioned when we will become more advanced?

C

7 You have invented a pair of glasses which allow you to read people's thoughts.

1 Do you:
   a) use them just for yourself?
   b) use them to become extremely rich?
   c) destroy them and try to forget all about them?
2 How could they be used for good and bad purposes?

The Satichi Corporation wants to produce the glasses. This is their chief scientist's development programme. Study the schedule and say what *will have happened/will be happening* by:

a) 2007   b) 2015   c) 2025?

2000	Research begins.
2005	First pair of 'magic' glasses produced.
2006	First experiments with 'magic' glasses.
2008	Mass production of 'magic' glasses.
2010	Every policeman has a pair.
2015	10 million pairs sold.
2020	20% of all families have a pair.
2025	Satichi Corporation invents a 'thought protection device' against the 'magic' glasses.

READING

8 Look at three further scenarios. They are written as though we are *already* in 2025. Which one, A, B or C, describes the following?

1 The end of human society as we know it.
2 The most peaceful world society.
3 The longest life expectancy for the rich.
4 The most dramatic developments in science.
5 The situation closest to Bruce Sterling's prediction.

A There hasn't been a world war since 1946. Reason and diplomacy have defeated madness and war. Nuclear weapons are a thing of the past, as are extreme ideologies. An international peace-keeping force has nothing more dangerous than rifles and bullets. Trade is freer and fairer so 'third world' countries have become much richer. Global life expectancy has risen to eighty-three years. New plants and genetic engineering have defeated famine and disease. The world's population is stable. People drive cars powered by solar energy and the tides. Natural balance has been restored to the environment and global warming is no longer a threat.

B The world is divided into three self-contained wealthy trading blocks: Europe, Spanish-speaking North and South America, and the countries of the Pacific rim. Other areas of the world still suffer to a certain extent from hunger and poverty. Europe is the richest of the three blocks since the destruction of Tokyo and San Francisco in the earthquakes of 2017. Although nuclear weapons still exist, treaties between the three blocks have made war unlikely. Advances in medicine mean that the rich can live to 130; however, life expectancy has fallen to fifty years in many parts of the world. Low-lying countries are in danger of floods caused by global warming, but world-wide political co-operation means that solutions are being found to environmental problems.

C The world is exhausted after a religious war which has claimed the lives of a billion soldiers and civilians. Parts of the world are nuclear wastelands. The chance discovery of a vaccine for AIDS has come too late to save the population of Central Africa. Unknown to humans, a fleet of spacecraft carrying extra-terrestrials is on its way to Earth. Within five years the population has been reduced by three quarters with its survivors living in slavery.

Hell or Utopia? Hell or Utopia? Hell or Utopia?

WRITING

9 Work in groups. Make notes about what you think will be happening in, or will have happened by, the year 2025. Consider the following areas:

• politics   • the world economy   • life expectancy
• medical science   • the environment

10 Using the scenarios above as a guide, write your own scenario from the standpoint of the present looking into the future. Use the future perfect and the future progressive tenses.

Sleeping visions

GETTING STARTED

1 Find out if anyone in the class has ever had a 'psychic' experience, such as a premonition.

Focus

TOPIC
• Premonitions

GRAMMAR
• Inverted sentences

SKILLS
• Reading: short texts
• Speaking: a conversation

SPEECH PATTERNS
• Inverted sentences: stress

VOCABULARY DEVELOPMENT
• Words related to sleep

READING

2 Read four short stories about 'psychic' experiences.

1 Which story describes the worst disaster?
2 Which story mentions a bad dream?
3 In which story does someone believe they could have stopped something terrible from happening?
4 Which story involves a publication?
5 Which story concerns a person taking a risk?
6 Which story has nothing to do with sleep or dreaming?

A Titanic sinking predicted

IN APRIL 1912, the liner *Titanic* struck an iceberg and started to sink. There weren't enough lifeboats for all the passengers and crew so fifteen hundred people died in the freezing water of the Atlantic. Sitting in one of the lifeboats, one of the survivors remembered a book which had predicted the disaster. The book, by Morgan Robertson, bore a strange relationship to the facts of the real story. Not only did he name the ship *Titan*, but he predicted where the *Titanic* would sink.

B James hits jackpot!

James Bigson, a student at Oxford University, had a really strange dream in which he saw the names of two racehorses. When he woke up he found out that they were in races later that day. No sooner did he discover this than he rushed out and placed bets on both of them. The horses won! This was not an isolated incident. Over the next few years James had a number of similar dreams and won a lot of money.

C Air crash could have been avoided

ONE MORNING Valerie Spring woke up after an awful nightmare. She told her husband that she had seen an air crash between two aircraft on a runway. She realised that the crash was at Tenerife airport. She was standing underneath the planes and people were screaming at her to help them. She told some of her friends about the dream, which tragically came true just seven days later. 587 people died. Never before had there been such a dreadful air disaster. For a long time afterwards she wished that she had been able to do something to prevent the accident from happening.

D Jewellery business: a gem!

Five years ago Mariano Miñot was getting bored in his safe and secure banking job in Mexico City. A friend invited him to start a new business manufacturing ethnic jewellery. He was tempted but realised there were risks not only for the career he had built but for his young family. After three sleepless nights an exhausted Mariano went to bed for an afternoon nap. Hardly had he fallen asleep when he had a terrible dream: he was locked in an empty, airless building and was suffocating. On waking he knew what he had to do and resigned from the bank. Five years later the jewellery business is highly successful.

3 Now answer these questions.

1 Which of the accounts do you think is the most frightening or sinister?
2 Can you logically explain one of these experiences?

DISCOVERING LANGUAGE

4 Look at these four pairs of sentences.

1 A *Not only did he name the ship* Titan, *but he predicted where the* Titanic *would sink.*

   B *He named the ship* Titan *and also predicted where the* Titanic *would sink.*

2 A *No sooner did he discover this than he rushed out and placed bets on both of them.*

   B *As soon as he discovered this he rushed out and placed bets on both of them.*

3 A *Never before had there been such a dreadful accident.*

   B *There had never been such a dreadful accident.*

4 A *Hardly had she fallen asleep when she had a terrible dream.*

   B *A few minutes after she fell asleep she had a terrible dream.*

1 Is there a real difference in meaning between each pair?

2 Which of each pair is the more 'dramatic'?

3 Which of each pair is used more in writing? Which is used more in speaking?

4 What happens when we put the adverbs at the beginning of the sentences?

5 What happens to the auxiliary verb and the subject?

SPEECH PATTERNS

5 ▢ Listen to the pairs of sentences from Exercise 4. Which words are stressed?

6 Rephrase these sentences, using the negative adverbial in brackets and inversion.

1 Mariano left the bank as soon as he had had the strange dream. (no sooner)

2 They had never had such a strange feeling. (never)

3 The problem wasn't just that I lay awake for hours, it was also that I had nightmares. (not only)

4 As soon as we had fallen asleep the alarm went off. (hardly)

5 This was the first time that a premonition had saved so many lives. (never before)

7 ▢ Listen and check your answers. Then with a partner practise saying the rephrased sentences using the appropriate stress.

DEVELOPING VOCABULARY

8 Work in pairs. Do you know the meaning of these words? Use your dictionaries to check.

to doze   to be sleepy   to have a sleepless night   to sleep like a log   to be fast asleep   insomnia   not to sleep a wink   to snore   to have a nap   sleeping pills   sleepwalker   to wake up   nightmare   dream   to fall asleep

Which words and expressions are associated with:

1 a noise?   4 deep sleep?
2 a feeling of tiredness?   5 a short sleep?
3 being unable to sleep?

Not all the expressions fall into these categories.

9 Complete these sentences using a word or expression from Exercise 8.

1 I'm tired; I think I'll have a ..... for half an hour.

2 The children were so tired that they ..... in the car on the way back home.

3 After lunch father used to ..... in his armchair.

4 People say you should never wake a ..... up as it can give them a terrible shock.

5 Last night I didn't sleep a ..... . The man in the next room kept on ..... all through the night and I had a ..... night. I'm exhausted!

6 After the accident she kept on having the same terrible ..... . It got so bad she was almost afraid to close her eyes.

7 Maurice has terrible problems with ..... ; it takes him hours to get to sleep; he has had to ask his doctor for some ..... .

8 I had an amazing ..... last night; you were wearing a flowerpot on your head!

SPEAKING

10 Work in small groups. Ask and answer:

1 how many hours' sleep you normally have.

2 if anyone ever has trouble sleeping, or any good remedies for insomnia.

3 if anyone in the class, or a family member snores.

4 if anyone has had any interesting dreams or even nightmares!

5 if anyone has ever had any experience of sleepwalking or sleepwalkers.

Giving a persuasive talk

READING

1 You are going to read a poem called *Noah's Arc* by Roger McGough. Before you read, think about these questions.

1 Who was the original Noah and what did he do?
2 What kind of challenges would a modern-day Noah face? What would he have to do?

2 Study the glossary, then read the poem and answer these questions.

1 Why is the poem called *Noah's Arc*?
2 Who is speaking in the poem?
3 How does he feel about what is going to happen?
4 What kind of person is he?
5 How does the poem make you feel? Does it make you laugh? Does it make you feel afraid?

3 Read the poem again and discuss these questions.

1 How good do you think his preparations are?
2 Do you think he belongs to some kind of organisation?
3 What do you think the following people think about him: his wife, his children, his neighbours and his doctor?
4 Do you have people like this in your own country?

Noah's Arc

In my fallout shelter I have enough food
For at least three months. Some books,
Scrabble, and games for the children.
Calor gas and candles. Comfortable beds
And a chemical toilet. Under lock and key
The tools necessary for a life after death.
I have carried out my instructions to the
    letter.

Most evenings I am down here. Checking
    the stores,
Our suits, breathing apparatus. Cleaning
And polishing. My wife, bless her,
Thinks I'm obsessive – like other men
About cars or football. But deep down
She understands. I have no hobbies.
My sole interest is survival.

Every few weeks we have what I call DD
Or Disaster Drill. At the sound of the alarm
We each go about our separate duties:
Disconnecting services, switching off the
    mains,
Filling the casks with fresh water, etc.
Mine is to oversee everything before finally
Shooting the dog. (This I mime in private.)

At first the young ones enjoyed the days
And nights spent below. It was an adventure
But now they're at a difficult age
And regard extinction as the boring concern
Of grown-ups. Like divorce and
    accountancy.
But I am firm. Daddy knows best
And one fine day they'll grow to thank me.

FOCUS ON STYLE

4 Discuss the following questions.

1 Why does 'Noah':
   a) compare nuclear war to a party?
   b) say he feels like an astronaut?
   c) compare the world today with a person suffering from cancer?
2 How effective are these images ?

Beneath my bunk I keep an Armalite rifle
Loaded and ready to use one fine day
When panicking neighbours and so-called
   friends
Try to clamber aboard. The ones who scoff,
Who ignore the signs. I have my orders,
There will be no stowaways. No gatecrashers
At my party. A party starting soon.

And the sooner the better. Like a grounded
Astronaut I grow daily more impatient.
Am on tenterhooks. Each night
I ask the Lord to get on with it.
I fear sometimes He has forsaken us,
We His favourite children. Meek, drilled,
And ready to inherit an earth, newly-cleansed.

I scan the headlines, watch the screen.
A doctor thrilling at each fresh tumour:
The latest invasion, a breakdown of talks.
I pray for malignancy. The self-induced
Sickness for which there is only one cure:
Radium treatment. The final absolution.
That part of full circle we have yet to come.

GLOSSARY

fallout shelter: after a nuclear explosion there is 'fallout'. Fallout is a kind of nuclear rain. A **fallout shelter** is a hiding place, often underground, where people shelter until it is safe to go outside.

mime: to demonstrate the meaning of an action without using language.

stowaway: someone who hides (stows away) on a boat or a plane for a free journey.

gatecrasher: someone who goes to a party without being invited.

to be on tenterhooks: to be in an anxious or worried state of mind. *Before they received the examination results everyone was on tenterhooks.*

LAST NIGHT'S science-fiction film, X, about an explosion at a nuclear reactor, was so realistic that thousands of viewers thought it was true. They are now looking for a safe place to shelter. Unfortunately, there is only room for three people.

SPEAKING

5 Read this newspaper article and find out what people think has happened. Your teacher has a small bunker with room for three people.

READING

6 📼 Read and listen to the talk below by a comedian who wants a place in the bunker.

1 How good do you think her arguments are?
2 Would they convince you?

❝I think you should let me into the bunker. After all, everyone is going to be sad and miserable and we'll all get terribly depressed. We'll need to stay optimistic and cheerful. Even though I can't cook or make things, I can keep everyone happy by telling them jokes and organising sketches. In difficult situations morale is very important. The last person we want with us is a politician or a soldier. They're the people who got us into the mess in the first place.❞

7 Now read the talk again carefully and answer these questions.

1 What reasons does the comedian give in her own favour?
2 How does she deal with the negative (i.e. not being able to cook or make anything)?
3 What does she say she can do?
4 Who does she think shouldn't be selected? What reason does she give?

8 Everyone in your class saw the film reviewed in the newspaper article above and believes it is true. Choose a role from below. You will have to give a short talk to persuade the others to let you have one of the places in the bunker!

doctor electrician mechanic soldier chef chemist poet university professor actor priest/sister policeman carpenter

9 Using what the comedian says as a guide, prepare your talk.

Grammar reference

1 The future perfect

- We use the future perfect to predict that an action will already be completed at a particular time in the future. This tense is often used with time expressions with *by*, which means 'at or before'.
  EXAMPLES: *I will have written my essay **by lunchtime**, but I won't have finished typing it.*
  *Will the lesson have finished **by eight o'clock**?*

FORM

- The form of the future perfect is:
  will + *have* + past participle
- Other common time expressions used with the future perfect are:
  By tomorrow morning/afternoon, etc.
  By this time tomorrow/next week/next year
  By (the year) 2025
  In five years' time
  Ten years from now
- The future perfect is often used to predict that something will already be completed when something else happens in the future.
  EXAMPLES: *When you see me again, I**'ll have grown** a beard.*
  *Next time you come to stay, we**'ll have had** central heating put in.*

  Compare this with the use of the future progressive (see Grammar reference 12.3):
  *When you see me again, I**'ll be wearing** contact lenses.*
- If we are not certain about our predictions, we use *may* or *might* instead of *will*.
  EXAMPLE: *By the year 2010, they **might have found** a cure for cancer.*

2 Inversion

- Inversion is a sentence pattern where we put a verb before its subject. A very common use is in short statements of agreement.
  EXAMPLES: *They can swim. So **can we**.*
  *I don't like cheese. Neither **do I**.*
  *I've finished my homework. So **have I**.*
- We sometimes use inversion after certain expressions of 'negative force': *Not only, Never, No sooner, Hardly*. We do this to add emphasis and usually only in very formal or literary written English.
  EXAMPLES: ***Not only did he** name the ship Titan, but he (also) predicted where it would sink.*
  ***Never** (before) **had there** been such a terrible accident.*

No sooner did he dream about the horses than he rushed out and placed bets on them.
Hardly had he fallen asleep when he had a terrible dream.

Note that we can only invert with *never* when it has the meaning of 'in my life'. We do not invert when we use *never* as an adverb of frequency.

FORM

- The inverted verb must be either a modal, an auxiliary (*do* or *have*), or the verb *be*. So sometimes we have to add the auxiliary verb *do*:
  *I love strawberries. So **do I**. (NOT *So love I*.)*
  This rule is the same as for the use of auxiliaries in question tags (see Grammar reference 3.3).
- Notice these typical patterns:

  Not only + any verb tense + *but also* + related verb tense:
  ***Not only is he** a marvellous violinist, **but he also plays** the drums.*
  (= He is not only a marvellous violinist, but he also plays the drums.)

  Never (before) + present perfect/past perfect:
  ***Never before had she seen** such beautiful paintings.*
  (= She had never seen such beautiful paintings before.)

  No sooner + past simple/past perfect + *than* + past simple:
  ***No sooner had he insulted** her **than he regretted** it.*
  (= As soon as he had insulted her, he regretted it.)

  Hardly + past perfect + *when* + past simple:
  ***Hardly had** his head **touched** the pillow **when he heard** a loud bang.*
  (= His head had only just touched ...
  or ***No sooner had** his head **touched** ...)

Talkback

Time travellers

1 Work in pairs. Look at the photograph, which predicts how a typical American will look in the year 2050. Scientists put the photographs of fourteen models of different ethnic groups into a computer. After 65 hours this is the picture which emerged. She is 15 per cent Anglo-Saxon, 17.5 per cent Middle Eastern, 17.5 per cent African, 7.5 per cent Asian, 35 per cent Southern European and 7.5 per cent Hispanic.

© 1993 Time Inc. Reprinted by permission

2 Based on what you know about American society now, how accurate do you think the prediction in Exercise 1 will be?

1 What could happen to change it?
2 What will people from your own country look like in 2050?

3 Will they be any different from today?

3 Work in three groups. Each group will be transported into the future. Discuss the questions below.

Group 1: You will be 100 years in the future.
Group 2: You will be 500 years in the future.
Group 3: You will be 1,000 years in the future.

• What will people be wearing?
• What will people look like?
• What will the latest fashion be?
• Will the family still exist?
• Will society be more or less violent?
• How will people be living and working together?
• How will they communicate?
• What skin colour will people have?
• Will people's bodies have evolved in any way?
• Which will the most powerful country be?
• What will happen to transportation?
• How long will people expect to live?
• What will people be eating?
• Which animals will have become extinct?
• What will people be doing for fun?
• Will there be any new religions or beliefs?

4 When you have discussed the questions, find someone from each of the other groups and exchange your ideas.

5 Now imagine that a time traveller from the society you have visited comes back to our day and age.

1 What would they say about the differences between society in our time and theirs?
2 If they made a documentary, what things would they include?
3 What articles would they take back to their time to show what we are like today?

15 *Memories*

Thinking back

GETTING STARTED

1 Work in pairs. Discuss these questions.

1 What are your earliest childhood memories?
2 In a recent survey, 73 per cent of interviewees said their earliest memory was an unhappy one. Childhood accidents or getting lost in stores were very common. How true is this of your class?

LISTENING

2 Before you listen, answer these questions.

1 What are the five senses? Which do you think are the most/least important?
2 If you could have an extra sense, what would it be? What would you like to be able to do?

3 🔊 Juliet describes a trick her memory played on her a few years ago. Listen and answer the questions.

1 What was she reminded of and why?
2 How did the experience make her feel? What different emotions did she experience?
3 How did the experience make her change her opinion of the five senses?

DISCOVERING LANGUAGE

4 Look at this use of *would* from Juliet's story.

. . . its strong sweet perfume **would** *fill the garden.*

1 Does this phrase describe the past, present or future?
2 Did the event happen once or often?
3 Could we use *used to* instead of *would*?
4 Look at the sentences below.
   a) Which form, *would* or *used to*, can be used to describe both past actions and past states?
   b) Which form can only be used for past actions?

A *We* **would/used to** *sit in the garden.* (correct)
B *I* **used to** *have long hair in those days.* (correct)
C *I* **would** *have long hair in those days.* (wrong)

5 Work in pairs. Tell each other about a time in the past and the things that you *would/used to* do.

FOCUS ON FUNCTIONS

6 What is the difference between these pairs of sentences? Think about meaning *and* structure.

1 a) The strength of the feeling surprised me.
   b) What surprised me was the strength of the feeling.
2 a) It surprised me.   b) It did surprise me.
3 a) It did.   b) It really did.
4 a) Taste and smell aren't very important.
   b) Taste and smell aren't that important.

SPEECH PATTERNS

7 🔊 Listen to the b) sentences from Exercise 6 and underline the words which are heavily stressed. Then listen again and repeat.

8 Julius is discussing a TV documentary about the past. Change the words in *italics* to make them more emphatic.

❝It was a fascinating documentary. *I was interested in the way ordinary people lived. I was surprised that some people never took a bath in their lives.* Nowadays we have got lots of amenities like central heating and cars, *but they aren't necessary.* It was OK if you were rich. *I was disgusted by the way some rich people treated their servants*; some had to work fourteen hours a day.❞

FOCUS ON LITERATURE

9 📼 **Listen and read the poem, *Piano*, by D. H. Lawrence. Which lines of the poem does each picture illustrate?**

Piano

A

Softly, in the dusk, a woman is singing to me;
Taking me back down the vista of years, till I see
A child sitting under the piano, in the boom of the tingling strings
And pressing the small, poised feet of a mother who smiles as she sings.

B

In spite of myself, the insidious mastery of song
Betrays me back, till the heart of me weeps to belong
To the old Sunday evenings at home, with winter outside
And hymns in the cosy parlour, the tinkling piano our guide.

C

So now it is vain for the singer to burst into clamour
With the great black piano appassionato. The glamour
Of childish days is upon me, my manhood is cast
Down in the flood of remembrance, I weep like a child for the past.

GLOSSARY

dusk: that part of the evening when the light is failing

insidious: working in a secret and harmful way

weep: a fairly poetic way of saying *to cry*; to cry silently with tears

---

10 **Now read these sentences which express the ideas of the same poem in everyday English. Which of the lines of the poem do they go with?**

a) Her voice takes me back in time to when I was a child sitting by my mother's feet as she played the piano.

b) I no longer feel like an adult as I am drowned in childhood memories and I cry like a child for what has gone.

c) Although I try to resist, the power of her singing tricks me, making me wish I could once more experience being at home in our small warm and comfortable living room.

d) As night falls I am listening to a woman singing.

e) It's a waste of time for the singer and piano to play loudly because I am lost in the happy sensations of childhood.

DEVELOPING VOCABULARY

11 **Find words in the poem which describe sound and music.**

SPEAKING

12 **Imagine that you are D. H. Lawrence describing to a friend in ordinary everyday English what happened to him. Use Juliet's story from Exercise 3 as a guide and add as much emphasis as you can.**

13 **Work in pairs. Describe an occasion when you were transported back in time by one of the senses.**

A mind like a sieve?

Focus

TOPIC
• Improving your memory

GRAMMAR
• *Always* for frequency
• *Always* + present progressive
• *Could always*

SKILLS
• Reading: articles
• Listening: a talk
• Speaking: role play

SPEECH PATTERNS
• *Always*: stress

GETTING STARTED

1 Work in groups. Discuss these questions.

1 How good are you at remembering things?
2 How do you memorise things like telephone numbers and lists of English irregular verbs?
3 Does anyone have any useful tips or techniques?

READING

2 Monica Andrews describes a way of memorising things which has changed her life. Read the introduction below and find out what problems she used to have at school.

❝Have you got a mind like a sieve? Mine used to be. Sometimes I would tie a knot in my handkerchief to help me remember something and then I would forget what the knot was for. My mother used to say: "You're always forgetting things!" Whenever I had more than three things to remember, my mind went blank. However hard I tried, nothing seemed to work. Whatever I did, writing things down or repeating them to myself, was hopeless.

I was in despair, until one day I found out about a simple way of remembering things which really works. It's this technique that I want to share with you by working through an example. It's called the number-rhyme system. You could always give it a try. Here's a list of ten words which I want you to study hard for a minute. Try to memorise them in the *same* order: table, feather, cat, leaf, student, orange, car, pencil, shirt and map.❞

When you think you know the list of words, test yourself with a partner!

DISCOVERING LANGUAGE

3 Read the introduction again and find sentences which mean the following.

a) Everything I did was hopeless.
b) Each time I had more than three things to remember my mind went blank.
c) It didn't matter how hard I tried, nothing worked.

Now answer these questions.

1 What kinds of word do the sentences you have found have in common? How does each word end?
2 Which sentences are more emphatic: those in the text or sentences a) to c)?

4 Rephrase these sentences, making them more emphatic.

1 I did everything to please him but he wouldn't forget.
2 If I go into any room in the house, there always seems to be a strange smell!
3 It didn't matter how hard I tried, it made no difference.
4 Everybody I ask agrees with me.
5 Everybody who comes on this course must have a degree.
6 He screamed as loudly as he could but nobody heard him.

LISTENING

5 You are going to hear how Monica's technique works. Before you listen, look at the pictures of ten objects and the numbers one to ten. Can you make any connection between the objects and the numbers?

vine   heaven
door   hen   shoe
bun   tree
sticks   gate   hive

1 2 3 4 5 6 7 8 9 10

6 📼 Listen and draw a line connecting the objects to the numbers. Had you already guessed the logic behind this?

READING

7 Read the rest of the talk and find out how to memorise lists of words like the list in Exercise 2.

❝Right, now you construct a strong mental image, including as many of the senses like taste and smell as you can, to connect each of the words in your list with the number-rhyme. For instance, word one, the 'bun' word on our list, was *table*; so we can imagine an enormous bun on top of a table, which is about to break because of the weight – smell the delicious aroma and taste your favourite bun! Word number two, the 'shoe' word, was *feather*. Right, so let's imagine your favourite shoe with an enormous feather growing out of it and tickling your foot so much you can't put the shoe on! Let's try another word further on, shall we? Word seven, the 'heaven' word, was *car*, wasn't it? So let's imagine all the angels sitting in cars rather than clouds, and experience driving the car that you think is heavenly! I think you've got the idea by now, haven't you? Spend a few minutes thinking of other images for the remaining words in your list. ❞

Look at the picture for word one. Then draw a picture for words number two and seven.

Work in groups and draw pictures which will connect the remaining number-rhymes with the other seven words. Then show them to each other.

8 Work in pairs. Use the number-rhyme system to help you remember this list of words.

kite   magazine   robot   mirror   dictionary
chimney   plant   telephone   computer   carpet

DISCOVERING LANGUAGE

9 Match these three sentences with the situations/comments below.

A   He **always** takes a taxi to work.
B   He's **always** taking a taxi to work.
C   He could **always** take a taxi to work.

- It really is an expensive habit.
- There is a bus strike and it's too far to walk.
- And I pick him up in the evening.

1   Which sentence implies a criticism?
2   Which sentence describes a habit or fact?
3   Which sentence describes a 'last resort' (what you do if all else fails)?
4   Which tense is used in each sentence?

SPEECH PATTERNS

10 📼 Listen to this sentence. Which word is stressed?

He's always taking my things.

Listen again and repeat. Imagine you are annoyed.

11 Using a construction with *always*, what would you say in these situations?

1   Your brother or sister often takes your clothes without asking permission. You're not pleased.
2   The last bus has gone and you don't want to walk home. You have enough money for a taxi.
3   Each day when you go to work you buy a newspaper at the station.

SPEAKING

12 Work in pairs.

Student A: You live in the centre of town near all the cinemas and entertainments. You are angry with your friend. He/She is either late for meetings or else arrives just before a film or play starts. You want your friend to be more reliable. You feel foolish about always being the one who has to stand outside waiting for him/her to arrive.

Student B: You are the friend. It is difficult for you to arrive at meetings on time because you live in the suburbs and don't have a car. You have to either take the bus or depend on one of your parents to give you a lift. You don't think it is fair that you always have to go into town. There are some good places for entertainment near you. You would like to take turns so that sometimes your friend comes to you.

Writing an essay (2)

Focus

TOPICS
- Childhood
- The environment
- Transport
- Foreign language learning
- Jobs for life

SKILLS
- Speaking: discussion/brainstorming
- Writing: planning an essay/a first draft/introductions/conclusions/second draft
- Reading: introductions, conclusions

STYLE
- Types of introductions and conclusions

READING

1 Read these notes about planning and organising.

When you write an essay you need ideas, vocabulary and an appropriate range of language and expressions to structure your arguments. In an examination, it is important to make sure that you have both the vocabulary and ideas before attempting to answer the question you have chosen. In Unit 13, you looked at an essay and the expressions that you can use. In this section we are going to look at ideas and vocabulary.

SPEAKING

2 Consider this essay title.

'Early childhood is the happiest time of our lives.' Discuss.

Look at this network diagram which shows the ideas and vocabulary the writer has brainstormed. Are there any areas missing from the network?

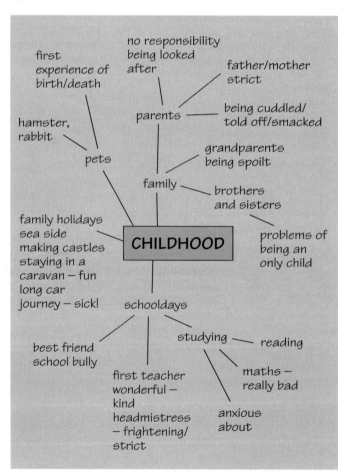

3 Now look at how we can change this into a plan. The plan is important because an essay has to follow a logical order.

PARAGRAPH 1
(Introduction)
- Define terms
- Childhood – 4 → 10

PARAGRAPH 2
Positive memories
- Childhood memories – many happy ones
- Lots of good things – no responsibility
- Grandparents spoilt me
- Holidays – great fun – staying in caravan; sandcastles

PARAGRAPH 3
Negative memories
- Difficult being only child. No brothers or sisters to play with, but best friend at school
- School worries – teacher wonderful but afraid of headmistress and school bully

---

PARAGRAPH 4
(Conclusion)
- Definitely happy (though not always), but the happiest?
- Different ages – different joys and problems

---

4 In pairs, make a network diagram for each of these two essays.

1 'Nowadays people worry too much about the environment.' Do you agree?
2 'It would have been better if the motor car had never been invented.' What do you think of this opinion?

5 Choose the diagram which has the most ideas and convert it into a four-paragraph plan. Make notes for each paragraph. Remember, Paragraph 1 is the introduction, and Paragraph 4 the conclusion.

WRITING

6 Still in your pairs, write the first draft of your essay. Only write Paragraphs 2 and 3. Don't write the introduction or the conclusion yet. You will use your essay for the rest of the exercises.

READING

7 Look at these essay titles and match them with the conclusions below.

1 'A job is not for life.' Summarise the arguments for and against staying in the same job for more than five years.
2 'Everyone should learn at least one foreign language.' Discuss.
3 Discuss the main problems of your town or region.

a) In conclusion, I feel that it is vital for all people to learn a foreign language, because in doing so they will be able to enrich their cultural lives. In my opinion, people who do not know a foreign tongue are the poorer for it. For this reason, the study of a foreign language should be compulsory until the age of eighteen.
b) To sum up, the main concerns I have are as follows: too much money is spent on new roads while public transport does not receive the funds it deserves. I recommend that money should be spent on improving public transport services in our town.
c) On balance, I think that a change every five years is of benefit to everyone. It seems to me that people's ideas could remain relatively fresh and that they are less likely to become inflexible. This change should be advantageous to both employer and employee.

FOCUS ON STYLE

8 Look at the conclusions in Exercise 7. Answer these questions.

1 Which words show that the writer has considered both the advantages and disadvantages?
2 Which words show that the writer is briefly restating his/her main points?
3 Which words indicate that this is the writer's opinion?
4 In which of the conclusions does the writer make suggestions?
5 How does the writer soften/strengthen what he/she thinks?

WRITING

9 Work in pairs. Write the conclusion for the essay you started in Exercise 6.

READING

10 Look at these introductions to the three essays in Exercise 7. To which essay does each introduction belong?

A Until about twenty years ago it was common for people to stay with the same company for years, even all their lives. The managing director may well have started his career as the boy who makes the tea and worked his way up through the company. In such a climate, changing jobs was not the 'done thing'. This is no longer the case.
B I consider transport to be the major problem in our town. In this essay I shall first describe the transport policy of our local government and then go on to assess its value.
C Let us consider the terms of the question. Who is 'everyone' in this situation? I am interpreting 'everyone' as people of an age able to learn. The term 'foreign language' I am taking to mean a language which is not spoken in one's own country. For instance, where I live we speak Basque at home and in my village, but Castillian is the official language of Spain.

Which introduction:

a) interprets the essay question?
b) says what will follow?
c) gives background information?

WRITING

11 Decide what type of introduction is suitable for your essay. Work in pairs. Write a first draft of your introduction.

12 When you have finished, edit your first draft with your partner and write a second draft.

125

Grammar reference

1 *Would* to describe past habits

- We can use *would* + infinitive without *to* in a similar way to *used to* (see Grammar reference 12.1) to talk about *habitual* past actions.
  EXAMPLES: *As soon as she got up in the morning, she **would make** herself a cup of tea.*
  *Charles **would** always **smoke** his pipe after dinner.*
  Notice that *always* comes in mid-position, between *would* and the main verb. Compare: *He always **used to smoke** his pipe.*
- Notice that *would* cannot be used to talk about past states. We have to use *used to*.
  EXAMPLE: *I **used to have** a pet parrot.* (NOT * *I would have a pet parrot.*)

2 *Wh -ever* words

- The words *whoever, whatever, whichever, whenever, wherever* and *however* are used as conjunctions to add emphasis, especially at the beginnings of sentences. The suffix *-ever* adds the meaning 'it doesn't matter':
  whoever = it doesn't matter who
  whatever = it doesn't matter what
  EXAMPLES: ***Whoever** he is, I'm too busy to see him.*
  ***Whatever** (else) you do, don't forget to take your passport.*
  ***Whenever** I smell baking bread, it reminds me of my childhood.*
  *Come out, **wherever** you are!*
  ***However** tired she felt, she was always patient and cheerful.*
  Notice that the two clauses are usually separated by a comma.
- *Wh -ever* words are also used as emphatic pronouns or adverbs, especially in questions.
  EXAMPLES: ***Whoever** can that be at this time of night?*
  ***Wherever** have you been? I've been really worried.*
  *I'll eat **whatever** I like.*
  ***However** did you manage to persuade her?*
  ***Whenever** did you find time to do that?*

3 *Always* with the present progressive

- *Always* can be used with the present progressive to express the idea that something happens very often or too often. It usually (but not always) means that we are complaining or criticising.
  EXAMPLES: *She**'s always borrowing** my clothes without asking me.*
  *Be quiet! You**'re always telling** me what to do.*
  *He**'s always buying** me flowers and chocolates.*
- *Always* can be used in the same way with the past progressive.
  EXAMPLE: *He **was always criticising** me.*

4 *Could always*

- The expression *could always* (+ infinitive without *to*) is used to suggest a solution to a problem. The word *always* does not have its usual meaning, but carries the idea of 'if everything else fails'.
  EXAMPLES: *You **could always write** to the manager and demand a refund.* (= Why don't you …)
  *We **could always take** a taxi.*
  Notice that this expression has a future meaning.
- *Could always* is often followed by *try* + the *-ing* form.
  EXAMPLE: *We **could always try phoning** for a taxi.*
- *Can always* is also possible and suggests that the action is more likely to happen.
  EXAMPLE: *If he phones, we **can always tell** him we're busy.*

Progress check Units 14–15

1 Complete these sentences with a suitable future form of the verb in brackets.

1 Come back tomorrow. Your photographs ..... (be) ready then.
2 This time next week I ..... (fly) over the Atlantic.
3 I think we ..... (finish) decorating the room by the time she comes out of hospital.
4 I'm sure they ..... (not find) a cure for cancer by the end of the century.
5 There's no point going to the supermarket. It ..... (close) by the time we get there.
6 Fine. I ..... (meet) you outside the station. But how ..... (I recognise) you? What ..... (you wear)?

2 Rewrite each sentence without changing its meaning. Begin with the words you are given.

1 The moment we got out of the car, our neighbour asked to speak to us.
  No sooner ...
2 She had never heard such a terrifying noise before.
  Never before ...
3 He was assassinated just as he stepped off the plane.
  Hardly ...
4 The burglars stole the jewellery, and also set fire to the valuable medieval tapestries.
  Not only ...

3 Choose a suitable response for each of the statements or questions. Do not use any response more than once.

I'm not that late!   Well, it did annoy me!
Wherever you like.   So do I.
You could always start without her.

1 I really like this restaurant.
2 Jane's always arriving late.
3 Where shall I sit?
4 So you finally decided to turn up!
5 Were you angry about his behaviour?

4 Fill each gap in this text with one suitable word.

I grew up in the country, one of a large family, and, [1]..... we were poor, I was [2]..... happy. My brothers and I [3]..... to walk three miles to school each day across the fields, [4]..... there was always something interesting to see or a new game [5]..... play.

  At certain times of the year, my father [6]..... go out hunting in the evenings and [7]..... usually take one of us children with him. [8]..... was the lucky one that day would [9]..... off proudly by Father's side. One of my earliest [10]..... is of crying because I was too young [11]..... go.

  If the hunting trip was a success, [12]..... had been caught [13]..... be cooked for supper the next day – usually one or two rabbits, or occasionally a duck. Even now, [14]..... I smell roast duck, I am transported back to those happy days of my [15]...... .

VOCABULARY

5 Complete each sentence with a word formed from the word in capitals.

1 Travelling to New York on Concorde was an ..... experience. (FORGET)
2 After several ..... nights, we asked the hotel management if we could move to a quieter room. (SLEEP)
3 The most ..... thing about our holiday was a walk by moonlight to the Temple of Poseidon. (MEMORY)
4 In most developed countries, life ..... for women is higher than for men. (EXPECT)
5 It's dangerous to drive when you're feeling .... (SLEEP)
6 Bond ..... the address on the piece of paper, which he then tore up into tiny pieces. (MEMORY)

Exercises for Student B

Unit 2: Dos and don'ts, Exercise 9
Ask and answer about rules and duties.

You have just joined a new college or job. Ask A what the rules are about: what to wear, being late, homework and behaviour. Tell A about the place you have just left, which was very free with no strict rules about clothes and with a flexible attitude to time and lateness.

Unit 2: Different systems, Exercise 7
Look at the chart. Explain it to A. Then answer his/her questions.

HIGHER EDUCATION IN ENGLAND AND WALES	

No. of students in Higher Education:
    now:
    10 years ago:
	$1/3$ of all school students
	$1/5$ of all students

Places of study:	colleges and universities
Entrance requirements:	2 'A' level passes
Fees:	paid by Government
Length of course:	*3 years for BA or BSc 4 years for MA
* Students studying a foreign language usually spend an additional year abroad.	

Unit 3: Come fly with me! Exercise 9
You are the airline representative. Use these notes to prepare your reply. Be firm but polite.

• Departure information is the responsibility of the airport, *not* the airline.
• Vegetarian meals have to be ordered two days in advance.
• There was a problem with the cabin service because two of the cabin crew were very ill and were unable to work, and there was also a trainee on board. Remind the passenger that this was a *cheap* charter flight.
• Apologise for not having enough places in non-smoking. Did the passenger check in early enough?
• The passenger has lost his/her luggage. Ask what the bag looks like and if it had a label. There are some bags left and you will check.
• You cannot offer compensation for this flight. Offer a 10% discount on a *future* return flight.

Unit 6: Sporting legends, Exercise 11
You are a young sportsperson. Decide which sport you play. Here are some ideas to help you.

• You started to play when you were eight years old (a bit too late really). Your mother was a keen player and she was your coach.
• You want to represent your country at the next Olympic Games because you think you could win a medal, but this is unlikely as your sport is not considered important in your country. You don't have enough money to give up work and train full time. Your only chance is a rich sponsor.
• Your big disappointment was losing the national final. You were also injured because you took a stupid risk during one game.
• You have a partner but you don't plan to get married yet. When you finish your career you'd like to be an actor or have a fashion company.

Unit 8: When friends fall out, Exercise 9
Respond to your partner's sentences. Then read these sentences to your partner. Decide how you feel when you give the news.

1 I've just won £10,000.
2 Someone has stolen my car again.
3 I've just failed my driving test for the third time.
4 Chris and I are going to get married.
5 I came top of my class in my exams.
6 I can't get into my house. I've lost my keys.

Unit 8: When friends fall out, Exercise 13
Use these notes to argue your case and try to resolve the situation.

You know that your agreement with Tamara probably wasn't legal, and that you didn't share the money with Billy. You are willing to compromise with Tamara. You want to get half the money but you don't think it is possible. You'd be happy with £15,000 but would accept £10,000. You feel that you have been let down by Tamara, but you would like to be friends again.

Unit 9: And now the good news, Exercise 11
You are a passerby. Respond to your partner using these notes and the cues on page 73.

You don't agree with Martyn Lewis. You think that radio and TV news is there to report the facts and to keep people up to date with important world events. You were angry once about a lot of reporting of a new baby in the royal family when the story of a big earthquake in India had not been mentioned. You think that Martyn Lewis is just a newsreader and that it is not his responsibility to decide what should go on the news. It is not his job to protect the public from the facts.